The Social Confidence Guide

Self-help, Volume 8

Timothy Scott Phillips

Published by Arcane Horizons Publishing, 2024.

While every precaution has been taken in the preparation of this book, the publisher assumes no responsibility for errors or omissions, or for damages resulting from the use of the information contained herein.

THE SOCIAL CONFIDENCE GUIDE

First edition. December 3, 2024.

Copyright © 2024 Timothy Scott Phillips.

ISBN: 979-8230874843

Written by Timothy Scott Phillips.

Table of Contents

The Social Confidence Guide (Self-help, #8) 1

Chapter 1: Understanding Social Confidence 6

Chapter 2: The Psychology of Shyness.. 19

Chapter 3: Self-Awareness and Self-Esteem 29

Chapter 4: Developing Social Skills.. 41

Chapter 5: Overcoming Social Anxiety.. 53

Chapter 6: Building Self-Confidence 69

Chapter 7: Effective Conversation Techniques 81

Chapter 8: Non-Verbal Communication Mastery............................... 94

Chapter 9: Social Etiquette and Manners.. 104

Chapter 10: Networking and Building Relationships 117

Chapter 11: Public Speaking and Presentation Skills 128

Chapter 12: Handling Social Rejection and Failure 140

Chapter 13: Online Communication and Social Media.................... 150

Chapter 14: Continuous Improvement and Practice......................... 163

Chapter 15: Real-Life Success Stories 172

To everyone who has ever felt held back by shyness,

this book is for you.

May it guide you toward discovering your voice,

building meaningful connections,

and stepping confidently into the world.

To those who encourage and support others

on their journey to social growth,

your kindness makes all the difference.

Together, let's create a world where everyone feels heard, valued, and empowered.

Introduction

Overview of the Book's Purpose and Goals

THE WORLD WE LIVE IN today is more interconnected than ever before. Our personal and professional lives hinge significantly on our ability to communicate effectively and build strong, meaningful relationships. However, despite the apparent ease with which many navigate social interactions, countless individuals struggle with social confidence, battling shyness and anxiety that inhibit their social and professional growth. This book, "The Social Confidence Guide: Overcoming Shyness and Building Connections," aims to address these challenges head-on.

The primary purpose of this book is to provide a comprehensive guide for anyone looking to enhance their social confidence. Whether you are someone who finds social interactions daunting, struggles with starting and maintaining conversations, or feels anxious in social settings, this book will offer you practical strategies and insights to help you overcome these hurdles. By understanding the underlying psychology of shyness and social anxiety, developing key social skills, and practicing effective techniques, you can transform your social interactions and build lasting, meaningful connections.

This book is structured to be a step-by-step guide, starting with understanding the fundamentals of social confidence and gradually building up to more advanced techniques and strategies. Each chapter is designed to tackle a specific aspect of social confidence, providing both theoretical insights and practical exercises. By the end of this book, you should have a solid foundation in social skills and the confidence to engage in social situations with ease.

Importance of Social Confidence

SOCIAL CONFIDENCE IS a critical component of our overall well-being and success. It encompasses the belief in one's ability to navigate social interactions, form relationships, and communicate effectively. Here are some key reasons why social confidence is so important:

1. Enhanced Personal Relationships: Social confidence allows you to form and maintain healthy relationships with family, friends, and romantic partners. It helps you express your feelings, needs, and boundaries effectively, leading to more fulfilling and supportive relationships.

2. Professional Success: In the professional world, social confidence is crucial for networking, collaboration, and leadership. Confident individuals are more likely to take on challenging tasks, seek promotions, and build strong professional networks. Effective communication and interpersonal skills are often key differentiators in career advancement.

3. Mental Health and Well-being: High social confidence is associated with lower levels of social anxiety and depression. It fosters a sense of belonging and reduces feelings of loneliness. People who are socially confident are better equipped to handle social stressors and maintain a positive outlook on life.

4. Life Satisfaction: Socially confident individuals tend to have greater life satisfaction. They are more likely to engage in social activities, pursue hobbies, and have a robust support network. This sense of fulfillment and engagement contributes to overall happiness and quality of life.

5. Effective Communication: Social confidence enhances your ability to communicate clearly and assertively. It helps you listen actively, interpret non-verbal cues, and respond appropriately. These skills are essential in both personal and professional interactions.

6. Problem-Solving and Conflict Resolution: Socially confident individuals are better equipped to handle conflicts and challenges in relationships. They can approach disagreements with a constructive mindset, leading to more effective problem-solving and conflict resolution.

7. Personal Growth: Developing social confidence is a journey of personal growth. It involves stepping out of your comfort zone, facing fears, and building resilience. This process not only enhances your social skills but also contributes to overall self-improvement and empowerment.

Brief Discussion of Shyness and Its Impact on Life

SHYNESS IS A COMMON trait that affects millions of people worldwide. It is characterized by feelings of discomfort, apprehension, or fear in social situations, often leading to avoidance of such interactions. While everyone experiences shyness to some degree, it can become a significant barrier to personal and professional growth for many individuals.

Understanding Shyness

SHYNESS IS A COMPLEX interplay of genetic, environmental, and psychological factors. Some people are naturally predisposed to shyness due to their temperament, while others may develop it due to negative social experiences or upbringing. Key features of shyness include:

1. Self-Consciousness: Shy individuals often feel highly self-conscious and worry about how they are perceived by others. They may fear judgment, criticism, or rejection, leading to heightened anxiety in social situations.

2. Social Inhibition: Shyness can lead to social inhibition, where individuals hold back from expressing themselves or engaging in social interactions. This can result in missed opportunities for connection and growth.

3. Physical Symptoms: Shyness often manifests physically, with symptoms such as blushing, sweating, trembling, or a rapid heartbeat. These physical responses can further intensify feelings of anxiety and discomfort.

4. Negative Self-Perception: Shy individuals may have a negative self-image and low self-esteem. They might view themselves as socially inadequate or unworthy, reinforcing their shyness and reluctance to engage in social interactions.

Impact of Shyness on Life

THE IMPACT OF SHYNESS can be profound, affecting various aspects of life:

1. Social Relationships: Shyness can hinder the formation and maintenance of relationships. Shy individuals may struggle to initiate conversations, join social groups, or express their feelings, leading to feelings of isolation and loneliness.

2. Professional Opportunities: In the workplace, shyness can limit career growth. Shy individuals may avoid networking events, public speaking opportunities, or leadership roles, missing out on career advancement and professional development.

3. Academic Performance: Shyness can impact academic performance, especially in settings that require active participation, group work, or presentations. Shy students may avoid raising their hand in class, participating in discussions, or seeking help from teachers.

4. Mental Health: Chronic shyness is often associated with social anxiety disorder, which can significantly impact mental health. It can lead to persistent feelings of anxiety, depression, and low self-worth, affecting overall well-being.

5. Daily Activities: Shyness can interfere with daily activities that involve social interaction, such as shopping, dining out, or attending social events. This can lead to a restricted lifestyle and a lack of engagement in enjoyable activities.

Overcoming Shyness

OVERCOMING SHYNESS is possible with the right strategies and mindset. It involves understanding the root causes of shyness, challenging negative thoughts, and gradually building social confidence through practice. Here are some key steps to overcoming shyness:

1. Self-Reflection: Take time to understand your shyness and its triggers. Reflect on past experiences, identify patterns, and recognize how shyness affects your life.

2. Set Realistic Goals: Start with small, achievable goals to build social confidence. Gradually increase the complexity of social interactions as you become more comfortable.

3. Practice Exposure: Expose yourself to social situations regularly. Start with low-pressure settings and gradually work your way up to more challenging scenarios.

4. Challenge Negative Thoughts: Identify and challenge negative thoughts that contribute to shyness. Replace them with positive affirmations and realistic perspectives.

5. Develop Social Skills: Focus on developing key social skills such as active listening, effective communication, and non-verbal cues. Practice these skills in everyday interactions.

6. Seek Support: Consider seeking support from friends, family, or a therapist. Joining social skills groups or workshops can also provide valuable practice and feedback.

7. Celebrate Progress: Acknowledge and celebrate your progress, no matter how small. Each step forward is a victory in building social confidence.

Conclusion

This book is designed to guide you on a journey from shyness to social confidence. By understanding the importance of social confidence, recognizing the impact of shyness, and applying practical strategies, you can transform your social interactions and build meaningful connections. The chapters ahead will provide you with the knowledge, tools, and motivation to overcome shyness and develop the social confidence needed to thrive in personal and professional life. As you embark on this journey, remember that social confidence is not an innate trait but a skill that can be developed with practice and perseverance. Let's begin this journey together, step by step, towards a more confident and connected you.

Chapter 1: Understanding Social Confidence

Definition of Social Confidence

Social confidence, also referred to as social self-efficacy, is the belief in one's ability to engage successfully in social interactions. It involves feeling comfortable and at ease in social settings, being able to initiate and maintain conversations, and effectively navigating various social contexts. Social confidence is not merely the absence of shyness but a proactive, positive feeling about one's social skills and interpersonal abilities.

Social confidence is built on several key components:

1. Self-awareness: Understanding one's own emotions, strengths, and weaknesses in social settings.

2. Self-esteem: Having a positive self-view and believing in one's worth.

3. Social skills: The ability to communicate effectively, read social cues, and respond appropriately.

4. Experience: Exposure to a variety of social situations that help refine and reinforce social skills.

A socially confident individual can effectively manage social anxiety, make strong first impressions, build and maintain relationships, and handle social challenges with ease.

The Impact of Social Confidence on Personal and Professional Life

SOCIAL CONFIDENCE PLAYS a critical role in both personal and professional spheres, influencing various aspects of life.

Personal Life:

1. RELATIONSHIPS: SOCIAL confidence helps in forming and maintaining healthy relationships. Confident individuals are better at expressing their needs, resolving conflicts, and providing emotional support.

2. Mental Health: High social confidence is associated with lower levels of social anxiety and depression. It fosters a sense of belonging and reduces feelings of loneliness.

3. Life Satisfaction: People with high social confidence tend to have greater life satisfaction. They are more likely to engage in social activities, pursue hobbies, and have a robust support network.

Professional Life:

1. CAREER ADVANCEMENT: Social confidence is crucial in the workplace. It aids in networking, public speaking, and leadership. Confident employees are more likely to take on challenging tasks and seek promotions.

2. Collaboration: Effective teamwork requires strong interpersonal skills. Socially confident individuals can communicate clearly, listen actively, and work well with diverse teams.

3. Conflict Resolution: In professional settings, conflicts are inevitable. Social confidence enables individuals to address disagreements constructively, fostering a harmonious work environment.

Common Misconceptions About Social Skills and Shyness

THERE ARE SEVERAL MISCONCEPTIONS surrounding social skills and shyness that can hinder the development of social confidence.

Misconception 1: Social Confidence is Inherent

MANY PEOPLE BELIEVE that social confidence is an innate trait that one either has or doesn't have. While some individuals may naturally be more outgoing, social confidence is largely a learned skill. Through practice and exposure, anyone can improve their social abilities.

Misconception 2: Shyness Equals Lack of Confidence

SHYNESS AND LACK OF confidence are often conflated, but they are distinct. Shyness is a tendency to feel awkward or anxious in social situations, often due to fear of judgment. However, a shy person can develop social confidence through positive experiences and skill-building.

Misconception 3: Outgoing People are Always Socially Confident

BEING OUTGOING DOES not necessarily mean one is socially confident. Outgoing individuals may still experience self-doubt and anxiety in certain situations. Social confidence is about the quality of interactions, not just the quantity.

Misconception 4: Social Confidence Means Being the Center of Attention

SOCIAL CONFIDENCE DOES not require one to be the life of the party. It involves being comfortable in one's own skin and engaging meaningfully with others, whether in small groups or large gatherings.

Misconception 5: Social Skills are Only Important in Social Settings

SOCIAL SKILLS ARE ESSENTIAL in all aspects of life, including professional environments. They enhance teamwork, leadership, and customer relations, making them invaluable in the workplace.

Building Social Confidence

BUILDING SOCIAL CONFIDENCE involves several steps:

1. Self-Reflection: Understand your current level of social confidence, identify areas for improvement, and recognize your strengths.

2. Skill Development: Focus on specific social skills such as active listening, effective communication, and empathy.

3. Practice: Engage in social situations regularly to practice and refine your skills.

4. Feedback: Seek constructive feedback from trusted friends or mentors to improve your social interactions.

5. Positive Reinforcement: Acknowledge and celebrate your progress to build confidence and motivation.

In-Depth Exploration of Social Confidence

TO TRULY GRASP SOCIAL confidence, it's essential to delve into its nuanced aspects. Social confidence isn't just about being able to chat at a party or feel at ease in meetings. It's about creating an authentic connection with others, understanding the subtleties of social cues, and navigating the complexities of human interaction.

Self-Awareness and Social Confidence

SELF-AWARENESS IS THE cornerstone of social confidence. It involves recognizing your emotions, understanding how they influence your behavior, and perceiving how others see you. People who are self-aware are better at regulating their emotions and are less likely to be overwhelmed in social situations. They can observe their interactions without being overly critical or anxious, allowing them to adapt their behavior to fit the context.

To build self-awareness, start with reflection. After social interactions, consider what went well and what didn't. Think about how your feelings influenced your behavior and how others responded. Mindfulness practices, such as meditation, can also enhance self-awareness by helping you stay present and observe your thoughts and emotions without judgment.

Self-Esteem and Social Confidence

SELF-ESTEEM PLAYS A significant role in social confidence. High self-esteem means valuing yourself and believing in your abilities, which naturally translates to more confident social interactions. If you have high self-esteem, you're less likely to fear judgment or rejection because you have a stable sense of self-worth.

Building self-esteem involves challenging negative self-talk and replacing it with positive affirmations. Surround yourself with supportive people who uplift you and remind you of your strengths. Engage in activities that you enjoy and excel at to reinforce your sense of competence and worth.

Social Skills: The Building Blocks of Confidence

DEVELOPING SOCIAL SKILLS is a fundamental aspect of building social confidence. These skills include verbal communication, non-verbal communication, active listening, empathy, and the ability to read social cues.

Verbal Communication

EFFECTIVE VERBAL COMMUNICATION is about more than just speaking clearly. It involves choosing the right words, tone, and style to convey your message. Practice speaking with clarity and confidence. Use positive language and avoid negative or self-deprecating remarks. Storytelling is a powerful tool in verbal communication; it makes conversations more engaging and memorable.

Non-Verbal Communication

NON-VERBAL CUES OFTEN speak louder than words. Your body language, facial expressions, and eye contact can significantly impact how your message is received. Practice maintaining an open posture, making eye contact, and using gestures to emphasize points. Pay attention to others' non-verbal cues to gauge their reactions and adjust your behavior accordingly.

Active Listening

ACTIVE LISTENING IS a crucial social skill that involves fully focusing on the speaker, understanding their message, and responding thoughtfully. To practice active listening, give the speaker your full attention, nod to show understanding, and provide feedback by paraphrasing or asking questions. Avoid interrupting or planning your response while the other person is speaking.

Empathy

Empathy, the ability to understand and share the feelings of others, is essential for building connections. Practice putting yourself in others' shoes and consider their perspectives and emotions. Empathy fosters trust and makes others feel valued and understood.

Reading Social Cues

SOCIAL CUES ARE THE subtle signals people give through their body language, tone of voice, and behavior. Being attuned to these cues helps you respond appropriately and navigate social interactions more effectively. Practice observing people's reactions and adjusting your approach based on their signals.

Experience: The Best Teacher

EXPERIENCE IS ONE OF the most effective ways to build social confidence. The more you expose yourself to social situations, the more comfortable and skilled you will become. Start with low-pressure environments, such as small gatherings with friends or family, and gradually move to more challenging settings, like networking events or public speaking.

Remember, it's normal to feel nervous or make mistakes. View each interaction as a learning opportunity. Reflect on what went well and what could be improved. Over time, these experiences will build your confidence and competence in social settings.

The Psychology of Social Confidence

UNDERSTANDING THE PSYCHOLOGICAL underpinnings of social confidence can provide valuable insights into how to develop it. Social confidence is influenced by cognitive, emotional, and behavioral factors.

Cognitive Factors

OUR THOUGHTS AND BELIEFS play a crucial role in social confidence. If you believe you are socially awkward or uninteresting, this will affect your behavior and interactions. Cognitive-behavioral therapy (CBT) techniques can help challenge and reframe these negative beliefs.

Emotional Factors

EMOTIONS, PARTICULARLY anxiety and fear, can significantly impact social confidence. Learning to manage these emotions is essential. Techniques such as deep breathing, progressive muscle relaxation, and mindfulness can help regulate anxiety and promote calmness in social situations.

Behavioral Factors

OUR BEHAVIORS, SUCH as avoiding social situations, can reinforce a lack of confidence. Gradual exposure to social interactions, combined with positive reinforcement, can help build confidence. Behavioral experiments, where you test out new social behaviors in a controlled manner, can also be beneficial.

The Impact of Social Confidence on Personal and Professional Life

SOCIAL CONFIDENCE SIGNIFICANTLY impacts various aspects of our lives, from personal relationships to professional success. Let's explore these impacts in more detail.

Personal Life

Building Relationships

SOCIAL CONFIDENCE IS foundational to building and maintaining healthy relationships. Confident individuals are more likely to initiate conversations, express their needs and boundaries, and resolve conflicts effectively. This leads to stronger, more fulfilling relationships.

Mental Health

HIGH SOCIAL CONFIDENCE is associated with lower levels of social anxiety and depression. When you feel comfortable in social situations, you are more likely to engage with others, seek support when needed, and participate in activities that promote mental well-being.

Life Satisfaction

Socially confident individuals tend to have greater life satisfaction. They are more likely to engage in social activities, pursue their interests, and have a robust support network. This sense of connection and fulfillment contributes to overall happiness.

Professional Life

Career Advancement

IN THE PROFESSIONAL realm, social confidence is crucial for career advancement. Confident individuals are more likely to take on leadership roles, seek promotions, and engage in networking opportunities. They can effectively communicate their ideas, collaborate with colleagues, and build professional relationships.

Effective Teamwork

EFFECTIVE TEAMWORK requires strong interpersonal skills. Socially confident individuals can communicate clearly, listen actively, and work well with diverse teams. They contribute to a positive team dynamic and foster collaboration.

Conflict Resolution

CONFLICTS ARE INEVITABLE in any professional setting. Social confidence enables individuals to address disagreements constructively, find common ground, and reach resolutions that benefit everyone involved. This fosters a harmonious work environment and enhances productivity.

Common Misconceptions About Social Skills and Shyness

THERE ARE SEVERAL MISCONCEPTIONS about social skills and shyness that can hinder the development of social confidence. Let's address these misconceptions and provide a clearer understanding.

Misconception 1: Social Confidence is Inherent

Many people believe that social confidence is an innate trait that one either has or doesn't have. While some individuals may naturally be more outgoing, social confidence is largely a learned skill. Through practice and exposure, anyone can improve their social abilities.

Misconception 2: Shyness Equals Lack of Confidence

Shyness and lack of confidence are often conflated, but they are distinct. Shyness is a tendency to feel awkward or anxious in social situations, often due to fear of judgment. However, a shy person can develop social confidence through positive experiences and skill-building.

Misconception 3: Outgoing People are Always Socially Confident

Being outgoing does not necessarily mean one is socially confident. Outgoing individuals may still experience self-doubt and anxiety in certain situations. Social confidence is about the quality of interactions, not just the quantity.

Misconception 4: Social Confidence Means Being the Center of Attention

Social confidence does not require one to be the life of the party. It involves being comfortable in one's own skin and engaging meaningfully with others, whether in small groups or large gatherings.

Misconception 5: Social Skills are Only Important in Social Settings

Social skills are essential in all aspects of life, including professional environments. They enhance teamwork, leadership, and customer relations, making them invaluable in the workplace.

Building Social Confidence

BUILDING SOCIAL CONFIDENCE involves several steps. It's a gradual process that requires self-reflection, skill development, practice, and positive reinforcement.

Self-Reflection

SELF-REFLECTION IS the first step in building social confidence. It involves understanding your current level of social confidence, identifying areas for improvement, and recognizing your strengths. Reflect on past social interactions, consider what went well and what could be improved, and set realistic goals for growth.

Skill Development

DEVELOPING SOCIAL SKILLS is crucial for building social confidence. Focus on specific skills such as active listening, effective communication, and empathy. Practice these skills in everyday interactions, and seek feedback from trusted friends or mentors.

Practice

Regular practice is essential for building social confidence. Engage in social situations regularly to practice and refine your skills. Start with low-pressure environments, such as small gatherings with friends or family, and gradually move to more challenging settings.

Feedback

Feedback is a valuable tool for improving social confidence. Seek constructive feedback from trusted friends, family, or mentors to gain insights into your social interactions. Use this feedback to make adjustments and continue improving.

Positive Reinforcement

POSITIVE REINFORCEMENT is crucial for building confidence and motivation. Acknowledge and celebrate your progress, no matter how small. Each step forward is a victory in building social confidence.

In-Depth Techniques for Building Social Confidence

LET'S DELVE INTO SOME specific techniques that can help you build social confidence.

Visualization

Visualization involves imagining yourself successfully navigating social interactions. This technique can help reduce anxiety and build confidence. Before a social event, spend a few minutes visualizing yourself engaging in conversations, making a positive impression, and feeling confident.

Positive Affirmations

POSITIVE AFFIRMATIONS are statements that reinforce your self-worth and confidence. Create a list of affirmations, such as "I am confident in social situations" or "I am a good communicator," and repeat them daily. Over time, these affirmations can help shift your mindset and build confidence.

Role-Playing

ROLE-PLAYING INVOLVES practicing social interactions in a controlled setting. Partner with a friend or mentor and simulate various social scenarios. This practice can help you build confidence and refine your social skills.

Exposure Therapy

EXPOSURE THERAPY INVOLVES gradually exposing yourself to social situations that cause anxiety. Start with low-pressure environments and gradually work your way up to more challenging settings. Each successful interaction will build your confidence and reduce anxiety.

Mindfulness and Relaxation Techniques

MINDFULNESS AND RELAXATION techniques can help reduce anxiety and promote calmness in social situations. Practice deep breathing, progressive muscle relaxation, or mindfulness meditation to manage anxiety and stay present during interactions.

Social Skills Training

SOCIAL SKILLS TRAINING involves learning and practicing specific social behaviors. This training can be done through workshops, classes, or self-help books. Focus on developing key skills such as active listening, effective communication, and empathy.

Seeking Professional Help

IF SHYNESS OR SOCIAL anxiety significantly impacts your life, consider seeking professional help. A therapist or counselor can provide valuable support and guidance. Cognitive-behavioral therapy (CBT) is particularly effective for treating social anxiety.

Conclusion

Understanding social confidence is the first step toward improving it. By dispelling common misconceptions and recognizing the impact of social confidence on various aspects of life, individuals can take proactive steps to enhance their social skills. With practice and perseverance, anyone can develop the social confidence needed to thrive in personal and professional settings. The chapters ahead will provide you with the knowledge, tools, and motivation to overcome shyness and build social confidence. Let's embark on this journey together, step by step, towards a more confident and connected you.

Chapter 2: The Psychology of Shyness

What is Shyness?

Shyness is a complex emotional state that encompasses feelings of discomfort, nervousness, and apprehension in social situations. It often manifests as a reluctance to engage in social interactions and can lead to significant emotional and behavioral consequences. At its core, shyness is characterized by an acute self-consciousness and a preoccupation with how one is perceived by others.

Shyness is not a one-size-fits-all phenomenon; it varies widely among individuals. Some may experience mild shyness that only emerges in specific situations, while others may feel intense shyness that pervades most of their social interactions. Common signs of shyness include:

- Avoidance of Social Situations: Shy individuals often go out of their way to avoid social gatherings or interactions.

- Physical Symptoms: Shyness can trigger physical responses such as blushing, sweating, trembling, or a racing heart.

- Difficulty in Communication: Shy people may struggle with starting or maintaining conversations, making eye contact, or expressing themselves clearly.

- Negative Self-Perception: Shy individuals often have a poor self-image and worry excessively about being judged or rejected by others.

Despite these challenges, shyness is not inherently negative. Many shy individuals are introspective, empathetic, and thoughtful, qualities that can be highly valuable. However, when shyness becomes a barrier to achieving personal or professional goals, it may be beneficial to seek strategies to manage and overcome it.

Causes of Shyness: Genetic, Environmental, and Psychological Factors

SHYNESS ARISES FROM a combination of genetic, environmental, and psychological factors. Understanding these underlying causes can provide insight into why some people are more prone to shyness and how it can be addressed.

Genetic Factors

RESEARCH SUGGESTS THAT genetics play a significant role in shyness. Studies of twins and families have shown that shyness can be heritable. Specific genes associated with the regulation of neurotransmitters, such as serotonin and dopamine, are thought to influence temperament and behavior, contributing to shyness.

- Temperament: From a young age, some children exhibit temperamental traits such as behavioral inhibition, which is closely related to shyness. These children may react with heightened sensitivity to new or unfamiliar situations, showing signs of distress or withdrawal.

- Neurobiological Factors: Brain structure and function also contribute to shyness. The amygdala, a region of the brain involved in processing fear and emotional responses, may be more reactive in shy individuals, leading to heightened anxiety in social situations.

Environmental Factors

ENVIRONMENTAL INFLUENCES, particularly during childhood and adolescence, significantly shape the development of shyness. Key environmental factors include:

- Parenting Styles: Overprotective or controlling parenting can contribute to shyness. Children who are not encouraged to explore and engage with their environment may develop a heightened sense of fear and dependency. Conversely, harsh or critical parenting can also foster shyness by damaging a child's self-esteem and confidence.

- Early Social Experiences: Negative social experiences, such as bullying, rejection, or criticism, can lead to shyness. Children who are frequently teased or excluded by their peers may develop a fear of social interactions.

- Cultural Influences: Cultural norms and expectations regarding social behavior can impact shyness. In some cultures, modesty and reticence are valued, while in others, extroversion and assertiveness are encouraged. These cultural differences can shape an individual's comfort level in social situations.

Psychological Factors

PSYCHOLOGICAL FACTORS, including cognitive and emotional processes, play a crucial role in the development and maintenance of shyness. These factors include:

- Self-Esteem and Self-Concept: Low self-esteem and a negative self-concept are closely linked to shyness. Individuals who perceive themselves as inadequate or unworthy are more likely to experience anxiety in social situations.

- Fear of Negative Evaluation: A core component of shyness is the fear of being judged or rejected by others. This fear can lead to heightened self-consciousness and avoidance behaviors.

- Social Skills Deficits: Some individuals may lack the social skills necessary to navigate social interactions confidently. This can create a cycle of negative experiences and increased shyness.

- Cognitive Distortions: Shy individuals often engage in cognitive distortions, such as catastrophizing (expecting the worst outcome) and mind-reading (assuming others are thinking negatively about them). These distorted thoughts can exacerbate feelings of anxiety and discomfort.

The Relationship Between Shyness and Social Anxiety

SHYNESS AND SOCIAL anxiety are closely related but distinct concepts. While both involve discomfort in social situations, they differ in terms of intensity, impact, and underlying mechanisms.

Understanding Social Anxiety

SOCIAL ANXIETY, ALSO known as social anxiety disorder (SAD), is a more severe and pervasive form of social discomfort. It is characterized by an intense fear of social situations where one might be scrutinized or judged by others. This fear leads to significant distress and avoidance behaviors that interfere with daily functioning.

Key features of social anxiety include:

- Intense Fear: Individuals with social anxiety experience a heightened fear of embarrassment, humiliation, or rejection in social situations.

- Avoidance: To avoid the anxiety associated with social interactions, individuals may go to great lengths to avoid social situations, such as skipping classes, avoiding work functions, or isolating themselves from friends and family.

- Physical Symptoms: Social anxiety can trigger severe physical symptoms, including sweating, trembling, nausea, and panic attacks.

- Cognitive Distortions: Similar to shyness, individuals with social anxiety engage in cognitive distortions that exacerbate their fears and anxieties.

Overlap and Differences

WHILE SHYNESS AND SOCIAL anxiety share similarities, they differ in several key ways:

- Intensity: Shyness is generally less intense than social anxiety. Shy individuals may feel uncomfortable in social situations but can still function relatively well.

In contrast, social anxiety involves a level of fear and distress that significantly impairs daily functioning.

- Impact on Life: Social anxiety has a more profound impact on an individual's life. It can interfere with academic or occupational performance, hinder relationships, and lead to isolation and depression. Shyness, while challenging, typically has a less severe impact.

- Persistence: Social anxiety is more persistent and pervasive than shyness. While shyness may fluctuate depending on the situation, social anxiety tends to be a chronic condition that affects multiple areas of life.

Comorbidity

Shyness and social anxiety often co-occur with other mental health conditions, such as depression, generalized anxiety disorder, and substance abuse. Understanding this comorbidity is crucial for effective treatment and support.

Strategies for Overcoming Shyness and Social Anxiety

BOTH SHYNESS AND SOCIAL anxiety can be managed and overcome with the right strategies. These approaches often involve a combination of cognitive-behavioral techniques, skill development, and gradual exposure to social situations.

Cognitive-Behavioral Therapy (CBT)

CBT IS A HIGHLY EFFECTIVE treatment for both shyness and social anxiety. It involves identifying and challenging negative thought patterns and behaviors that contribute to social discomfort.

- Cognitive Restructuring: This technique involves identifying and challenging distorted thoughts, such as catastrophizing or mind-reading, and replacing them with more realistic and positive beliefs.

- Behavioral Experiments: CBT often includes behavioral experiments where individuals test out their fears in a controlled manner. For example, someone might engage in a conversation with a stranger to challenge their fear of rejection.

- Exposure Therapy: Gradual exposure to feared social situations helps individuals build confidence and reduce anxiety over time. Starting with less intimidating situations and gradually working up to more challenging ones can be effective.

Social Skills Training

DEVELOPING SOCIAL SKILLS is crucial for building confidence and reducing anxiety in social situations. Social skills training involves learning and practicing specific behaviors, such as active listening, assertiveness, and effective communication.

- Role-Playing: Practicing social interactions through role-playing can help individuals build confidence and refine their skills in a safe and supportive environment.

- Feedback and Reinforcement: Receiving constructive feedback from a therapist or support group can provide valuable insights and encouragement for improvement.

- Modeling: Observing and imitating socially confident individuals can also be beneficial. This technique, known as modeling, helps individuals learn appropriate social behaviors through observation.

Mindfulness and Relaxation Techniques

MINDFULNESS AND RELAXATION techniques can help manage the physical and emotional symptoms of shyness and social anxiety. These practices promote a state of calm and present-moment awareness, reducing the impact of anxiety.

- Mindfulness Meditation: Mindfulness meditation involves focusing on the present moment without judgment. Regular practice can help individuals become more aware of their thoughts and feelings and develop a more accepting and non-reactive stance toward them.

- Deep Breathing: Deep breathing exercises can help regulate the body's stress response and promote relaxation. Practicing deep breathing before or during social interactions can reduce physical symptoms of anxiety.

- Progressive Muscle Relaxation: This technique involves tensing and relaxing different muscle groups in the body to release tension and promote relaxation.

Building Self-Esteem

IMPROVING SELF-ESTEEM is essential for overcoming shyness and social anxiety. Higher self-esteem leads to greater confidence and a more positive self-concept.

- Positive Affirmations: Repeating positive affirmations, such as "I am capable" or "I am worthy," can help shift negative self-perceptions and build confidence.

- Setting and Achieving Goals: Setting small, achievable goals and celebrating successes can boost self-esteem and provide a sense of accomplishment.

- Engaging in Activities that Foster Competence: Participating in activities where individuals feel competent and successful can enhance self-esteem. This could include hobbies, sports, or volunteer work.

Seeking Professional Help

FOR INDIVIDUALS STRUGGLING with severe shyness or social anxiety, seeking professional help from a therapist or counselor can be highly beneficial.

Mental health professionals can provide tailored treatment plans and support to address specific challenges.

- Individual Therapy: One-on-one therapy sessions can help individuals explore the root causes of their shyness or social anxiety and develop personalized strategies for overcoming it.

- Group Therapy: Group therapy provides a supportive environment where individuals can practice social skills, share experiences, and receive feedback from peers.

- Medication: In some cases, medication may be prescribed to manage severe anxiety symptoms. This should be done under the guidance of a qualified healthcare professional.

Personal Stories and Case Studies

TO ILLUSTRATE THE IMPACT of shyness and social anxiety and the effectiveness of various strategies, let's explore some personal stories and case studies.

Case Study 1: Sarah's Journey to Overcoming Shyness

SARAH, A 28-YEAR-OLD graphic designer, had always struggled with shyness. Throughout her school years, she avoided social activities and found it difficult to make friends. In her professional life, her shyness continued to hold her back. She avoided networking events and rarely spoke up in meetings, despite having valuable ideas to contribute.

Sarah decided to seek help from a therapist who specialized in CBT. Through cognitive restructuring, she began to challenge her negative thoughts about herself and her social abilities. She also practiced exposure therapy by gradually attending more social events and engaging in conversations with colleagues.

With time and practice, Sarah's confidence grew. She started participating more actively in meetings and even took on a leadership role in a team project. Her improved social confidence also led to stronger relationships with her coworkers and a more fulfilling social life outside of work.

Case Study 2: Mark's Battle with Social Anxiety

MARK, A 35-YEAR-OLD teacher, experienced severe social anxiety. The thought of speaking in front of his class or interacting with parents caused him intense fear and physical symptoms such as sweating and trembling. His anxiety began to interfere with his teaching and personal life.

Mark's therapist introduced him to mindfulness and relaxation techniques, which helped him manage his physical symptoms of anxiety. He also participated in social skills training and role-playing exercises to build his confidence in social interactions.

Gradually, Mark's anxiety diminished. He felt more at ease speaking in front of his class and started enjoying interactions with parents and colleagues. His improved social confidence had a positive impact on his teaching effectiveness and overall well-being.

Personal Story: Emily's Transformation

EMILY, A SHY AND INTROVERTED college student, struggled to make friends and participate in class discussions. She often felt lonely and isolated, which affected her academic performance and mental health.

Determined to overcome her shyness, Emily joined a social skills group on campus. Through the group, she practiced active listening, assertiveness, and effective communication. She also received feedback and support from her peers, which boosted her confidence.

Emily's transformation was remarkable. She started forming meaningful friendships, participating more in class, and even joined a student organization. Her newfound social confidence enriched her college experience and set her on a path to success.

Conclusion

Shyness is a common emotional state that affects many individuals, but it does not have to be a lifelong barrier. By understanding the genetic, environmental, and psychological factors that contribute to shyness and recognizing the relationship between shyness and social anxiety, individuals can take proactive steps to manage and overcome these challenges.

With the right strategies, including cognitive-behavioral techniques, social skills training, mindfulness practices, and support from professionals, anyone can build social confidence. Personal stories and case studies demonstrate that transformation is possible, providing hope and inspiration for those struggling with shyness or social anxiety.

As you continue reading this book, remember that overcoming shyness is a journey that requires patience, perseverance, and self-compassion. By embracing this journey and applying the insights and techniques discussed, you can develop the social confidence needed to thrive in both personal and professional settings. Let's move forward together, step by step, towards a more confident and connected you.

Chapter 3: Self-Awareness and Self-Esteem

Importance of Self-Awareness in Social Interactions

Self-awareness is the foundation of emotional intelligence and social competence. It is the ability to recognize and understand one's own emotions, thoughts, and behaviors and how they influence interactions with others. In social interactions, self-awareness allows individuals to monitor their reactions, adjust their behavior, and communicate more effectively. This chapter delves into the importance of self-awareness in social interactions and provides practical techniques for increasing self-awareness and building healthy self-esteem.

Understanding Emotions and Reactions

SELF-AWARENESS INVOLVES a deep understanding of one's emotional landscape. Recognizing how different situations, people, and events trigger various emotional responses is crucial for managing these emotions effectively. For example, feeling anxious before a social event is a common experience. However, a self-aware person can identify this anxiety, understand its source, and implement strategies to manage it, such as deep breathing or positive self-talk.

Emotional self-awareness also includes recognizing how emotions influence behavior. When aware of feelings of anger or frustration, a person can choose to respond calmly rather than react impulsively. This ability to regulate emotions enhances social interactions by preventing misunderstandings and fostering positive communication.

Improving Social Interactions

SELF-AWARENESS PLAYS a pivotal role in improving social interactions. By understanding their own communication style, strengths, and weaknesses, individuals can tailor their approach to different social situations. For instance, a person who knows they tend to dominate conversations can consciously make an effort to listen more and encourage others to share their thoughts.

Furthermore, self-awareness helps individuals recognize their impact on others. Understanding how one's words and actions affect others' emotions and perceptions is essential for building and maintaining healthy relationships. This awareness fosters empathy, allowing individuals to respond to others' needs and emotions more effectively.

Enhancing Empathy and Understanding

EMPATHY, THE ABILITY to understand and share the feelings of others, is closely linked to self-awareness. When individuals are attuned to their own emotions, they are better equipped to recognize and understand the emotions of others. This empathetic understanding forms the basis for meaningful connections and effective communication.

Self-aware individuals can also recognize when their own biases or assumptions may influence their interactions. By acknowledging and addressing these biases, they can approach social interactions with an open mind and a genuine interest in understanding others' perspectives.

Building Trust and Authenticity

TRUST AND AUTHENTICITY are fundamental components of healthy social interactions. Self-awareness contributes to both by promoting honesty and transparency. When individuals are aware of their values, beliefs, and motivations, they can communicate authentically and build trust with others.

Authenticity involves being true to oneself while respecting the differences of others. Self-aware individuals are less likely to engage in behaviors that are inconsistent with their values or that compromise their integrity. This consistency fosters trust and strengthens relationships.

Techniques for Increasing Self-Awareness

INCREASING SELF-AWARENESS is a continuous process that involves self-reflection, mindfulness, and feedback from others. The following techniques can help individuals enhance their self-awareness and develop a deeper understanding of themselves.

Self-Reflection

SELF-REFLECTION IS the practice of examining one's thoughts, emotions, and behaviors to gain insight and understanding. Regular self-reflection can reveal patterns, triggers, and underlying beliefs that influence behavior. Journaling is a powerful tool for self-reflection. By writing about daily experiences, emotions, and interactions, individuals can identify recurring themes and gain clarity about their inner world.

Questions for self-reflection might include:

- What emotions did I experience today, and what triggered them?

- How did I respond to challenging situations or conflicts?

- What thoughts or beliefs influenced my behavior in social interactions?

- How did my actions affect others, and how did they respond?

Mindfulness Meditation

MINDFULNESS MEDITATION is a practice that involves focusing on the present moment without judgment. It helps individuals become more aware of their thoughts and emotions as they arise. By observing these experiences without attachment or aversion, individuals can develop greater self-awareness and emotional regulation.

A basic mindfulness meditation practice involves:

- Finding a quiet and comfortable place to sit.

- Closing the eyes and taking a few deep breaths to relax.

- Focusing attention on the breath, noticing the sensation of each inhale and exhale.

- When the mind wanders, gently bringing attention back to the breath.

- Practicing non-judgmental awareness, simply observing thoughts and emotions without trying to change them.

Seeking Feedback from Others

FEEDBACK FROM TRUSTED friends, family members, or colleagues can provide valuable insights into how one's behavior is perceived by others. Constructive feedback can highlight blind spots and areas for improvement that might not be evident through self-reflection alone.

When seeking feedback, it is important to:

- Choose individuals who are honest, supportive, and have your best interests at heart.

- Be open to receiving feedback without becoming defensive or dismissive.

- Ask specific questions about behaviors or situations you want to understand better.

- Reflect on the feedback and consider how it aligns with your self-perception.

Personality Assessments

PERSONALITY ASSESSMENTS, such as the Myers-Briggs Type Indicator (MBTI) or the Big Five Personality Traits, can offer insights into one's personality traits, preferences, and tendencies. These assessments can help individuals understand their natural inclinations and how they interact with others.

While personality assessments can provide valuable information, it is important to remember that they are tools for self-awareness, not definitive labels. Individuals are complex and dynamic, and self-awareness involves recognizing the full range of one's experiences and behaviors.

Mindful Journaling

MINDFUL JOURNALING combines mindfulness and journaling practices to enhance self-awareness. It involves writing about experiences and emotions with a mindful and non-judgmental attitude. This practice encourages individuals to explore their inner world with curiosity and compassion.

A mindful journaling practice might include:

- Setting aside a specific time each day for journaling.

- Writing about emotions, thoughts, and experiences without censoring or judging.

- Reflecting on the connections between emotions, thoughts, and behaviors.

- Exploring questions such as, "What am I feeling right now?" or "What thoughts are driving my actions?"

Developing Emotional Vocabulary

DEVELOPING A RICH EMOTIONAL vocabulary helps individuals articulate their feelings and understand their emotional experiences more precisely. Using specific and nuanced language to describe emotions can enhance self-awareness and communication.

For example, instead of saying, "I feel bad," individuals can identify specific emotions such as "I feel frustrated," "I feel anxious," or "I feel disappointed." This clarity allows for a deeper understanding of emotional experiences and more effective emotional regulation.

Practicing Active Listening

ACTIVE LISTENING INVOLVES fully engaging with others' words and emotions, which in turn enhances self-awareness. By listening attentively to others, individuals can gain insights into their own communication patterns and emotional responses.

Active listening practices include:

- Maintaining eye contact and showing genuine interest in the speaker.

- Reflecting back what the speaker says to ensure understanding.

- Asking open-ended questions to encourage deeper conversation.

- Being aware of one's own emotional reactions and responses during the conversation.

Building and Maintaining Healthy Self-Esteem

SELF-ESTEEM IS THE overall sense of value and self-worth that individuals hold about themselves. Healthy self-esteem is crucial for social confidence and well-being. It involves having a positive self-view, recognizing one's strengths and achievements, and maintaining resilience in the face of challenges.

Understanding Self-Esteem

SELF-ESTEEM CAN BE conceptualized as existing on a spectrum, ranging from low to high. Individuals with low self-esteem may struggle with self-doubt, negative self-perception, and a lack of confidence. Conversely, individuals with high self-esteem have a positive self-view, feel confident in their abilities, and are resilient in the face of setbacks.

Healthy self-esteem is characterized by:

- A balanced and realistic self-view, recognizing both strengths and areas for growth.

- The ability to accept and learn from mistakes without being overly critical.

- A sense of self-worth that is not solely dependent on external validation or achievements.

- The capacity to set and pursue meaningful goals with confidence.

Factors Influencing Self-Esteem

SEVERAL FACTORS INFLUENCE the development and maintenance of self-esteem. These include:

- Early Experiences: Childhood experiences, including relationships with caregivers, significantly impact self-esteem. Supportive, nurturing, and validating environments foster healthy self-esteem, while critical or neglectful environments can undermine it.

- Social Comparisons: Comparing oneself to others can influence self-esteem. While healthy comparisons can motivate growth, constant or unrealistic comparisons can lead to feelings of inadequacy.

- Achievements and Successes: Personal achievements and successes contribute to self-esteem. Recognizing and celebrating accomplishments reinforces a positive self-view.

- Relationships: Positive relationships with friends, family, and peers provide validation, support, and a sense of belonging, all of which bolster self-esteem.

- Self-Compassion: Treating oneself with kindness and understanding, especially during times of failure or difficulty, is essential for maintaining healthy self-esteem.

Techniques for Building Healthy Self-Esteem

BUILDING AND MAINTAINING healthy self-esteem involves cultivating a positive self-view, recognizing strengths, and practicing self-compassion. The following techniques can help individuals enhance their self-esteem:

Positive Affirmations

POSITIVE AFFIRMATIONS are statements that reinforce a positive self-view and counteract negative self-talk. Regularly repeating affirmations can help shift one's mindset and build confidence.

Examples of positive affirmations include:

- "I am capable and confident in my abilities."

- "I deserve love, respect, and happiness."

- "I learn and grow from my experiences."

Setting and Achieving Goals

SETTING AND ACHIEVING meaningful goals can boost self-esteem by providing a sense of accomplishment and purpose. Goals should be specific, achievable, and aligned with one's values and interests.

When setting goals, it is important to:

- Break down larger goals into smaller, manageable steps.

- Celebrate progress and achievements along the way.

- Reflect on the skills and strengths developed through goal pursuit.

Recognizing and Celebrating Strengths

IDENTIFYING AND CELEBRATING one's strengths and achievements is crucial for building self-esteem. This practice involves acknowledging personal qualities, talents, and accomplishments, no matter how small.

Techniques for recognizing and celebrating strengths include:

- Creating a strengths inventory by listing personal qualities and skills.

- Keeping a "success journal" to document daily achievements and positive experiences.

- Seeking feedback from trusted friends or mentors to gain insights into one's strengths.

Practicing Self-Compassion

SELF-COMPASSION INVOLVES treating oneself with the same kindness and understanding that one would offer to a friend. It is especially important during times of failure or difficulty.

Self-compassion practices include:

- Recognizing that mistakes and setbacks are a natural part of the human experience.

- Offering oneself words of comfort and encouragement rather than criticism.

- Engaging in self-care activities that nurture one's physical, emotional, and mental well-being.

Challenging Negative Self-Talk

NEGATIVE SELF-TALK can undermine self-esteem and reinforce feelings of inadequacy. Challenging and reframing negative thoughts is essential for building a positive self-view.

Steps for challenging negative self-talk include:

- Identifying and acknowledging negative thoughts.

- Questioning the validity and accuracy of these thoughts.

- Replacing negative thoughts with positive and realistic statements.

Building Healthy Relationships

POSITIVE AND SUPPORTIVE relationships contribute significantly to self-esteem. Surrounding oneself with people who uplift, validate, and encourage personal growth is essential for maintaining a positive self-view.

Building healthy relationships involves:

- Seeking out friendships and connections that are based on mutual respect and support.

- Setting boundaries with individuals who are critical, toxic, or unsupportive.

- Communicating openly and honestly with friends, family, and peers.

Engaging in Activities that Foster Competence

PARTICIPATING IN ACTIVITIES that foster a sense of competence and mastery can enhance self-esteem. These activities provide opportunities to develop skills, achieve goals, and experience success.

Examples of such activities include:

- Pursuing hobbies and interests that align with one's passions and talents.

- Volunteering or engaging in community service to make a positive impact.

- Seeking out challenges and opportunities for growth in personal and professional life.

Practicing Gratitude

GRATITUDE INVOLVES recognizing and appreciating the positive aspects of one's life. Practicing gratitude can shift focus from negative thoughts and experiences to positive ones, enhancing overall well-being and self-esteem.

Gratitude practices include:

- Keeping a gratitude journal to document daily blessings and positive experiences.

- Expressing gratitude to others through words, gestures, or acts of kindness.

- Reflecting on moments of joy, success, and connection.

Personal Stories and Case Studies

TO ILLUSTRATE THE IMPACT of self-awareness and self-esteem on social interactions, let's explore some personal stories and case studies.

Case Study 1: Jane's Journey to Self-Awareness and Self-Esteem

JANE, A 30-YEAR-OLD marketing professional, struggled with low self-esteem and a lack of self-awareness. She often felt insecure in social situations and doubted her abilities at work. Jane's therapist introduced her to mindfulness meditation and journaling practices to enhance her self-awareness.

Through regular self-reflection and mindfulness, Jane began to recognize her negative self-talk and its impact on her behavior. She also started setting small, achievable goals and celebrating her progress. Over time, Jane's self-esteem improved, and she became more confident in her social interactions and professional abilities.

Case Study 2: Tom's Transformation through Feedback and Positive Affirmations

TOM, A 40-YEAR-OLD engineer, had always been critical of himself and struggled with negative self-talk. His low self-esteem affected his relationships and career growth. Tom decided to seek feedback from trusted colleagues and friends to gain insights into his strengths and areas for improvement.

The feedback Tom received highlighted qualities he had overlooked, such as his problem-solving skills and ability to collaborate effectively. He also started practicing positive affirmations daily. This combination of external feedback and internal affirmation helped Tom build a more positive self-view and enhanced his self-esteem.

Personal Story: Lisa's Path to Self-Compassion and Confidence

LISA, A 25-YEAR-OLD graduate student, was highly self-critical and struggled with perfectionism. She often felt overwhelmed by her academic and social responsibilities. Lisa's therapist introduced her to self-compassion practices, encouraging her to treat herself with kindness and understanding.

Lisa began practicing self-compassion by acknowledging her efforts and progress rather than focusing solely on her mistakes. She also engaged in self-care activities, such as yoga and journaling, to nurture her well-being. Over time, Lisa's self-esteem improved, and she developed a healthier, more balanced perspective on herself and her accomplishments.

Conclusion

Self-awareness and self-esteem are fundamental components of social confidence and overall well-being. By understanding the importance of self-awareness in social interactions and employing techniques to enhance self-awareness, individuals can develop a deeper understanding of themselves and their emotions. Building and maintaining healthy self-esteem involves cultivating a positive self-view, recognizing strengths, and practicing self-compassion.

Personal stories and case studies demonstrate that transformation is possible with the right strategies and mindset. As you continue reading this book, remember that self-awareness and self-esteem are ongoing journeys that require patience, practice, and self-compassion. By embracing these journeys and applying the insights and techniques discussed, you can develop the social confidence needed to thrive in both personal and professional settings. Let's move forward together, step by step, towards a more self-aware, confident, and empowered you.

Chapter 4: Developing Social Skills

Core Social Skills Needed for Effective Communication

Effective communication is the bedrock of strong relationships and successful interactions in both personal and professional contexts. Developing core social skills is essential for engaging in meaningful conversations, building rapport, and navigating social situations with confidence. This chapter explores the fundamental social skills necessary for effective communication and provides practical strategies for enhancing these skills.

1. Active Listening

ACTIVE LISTENING IS a crucial social skill that involves fully engaging with the speaker, understanding their message, and responding thoughtfully. It goes beyond hearing words; it requires paying attention to the speaker's verbal and non-verbal cues, showing empathy, and providing feedback. Active listening fosters trust, respect, and deeper connections in conversations.

2. Verbal Communication

VERBAL COMMUNICATION is the ability to convey thoughts, ideas, and emotions through spoken words. Effective verbal communication involves clarity, coherence, and the appropriate use of tone and language. It requires articulating thoughts clearly, using language that suits the context and audience, and adjusting speech patterns to ensure understanding.

3. Non-Verbal Communication

NON-VERBAL COMMUNICATION encompasses body language, facial expressions, gestures, posture, eye contact, and tone of voice. It plays a significant role in conveying emotions, intentions, and attitudes. Effective non-verbal communication enhances verbal messages, reinforces meaning, and helps interpret the unspoken elements of interactions.

4. Empathy

Empathy is the ability to understand and share the feelings of others. It involves recognizing and validating others' emotions, showing compassion, and responding with sensitivity. Empathy fosters connection, builds trust, and promotes effective communication by allowing individuals to see things from others' perspectives.

5. Assertiveness

Assertiveness is the ability to express oneself confidently and respectfully without being aggressive or passive. It involves standing up for one's rights, expressing needs and opinions clearly, and setting boundaries. Assertiveness contributes to healthy relationships and effective communication by promoting honesty and mutual respect.

6. Conflict Resolution

CONFLICT RESOLUTION skills are essential for managing disagreements and resolving disputes constructively. Effective conflict resolution involves active listening, empathy, problem-solving, and negotiation. It requires understanding different viewpoints, finding common ground, and working towards mutually beneficial solutions.

7. Emotional Regulation

EMOTIONAL REGULATION is the ability to manage and control one's emotions in various situations. It involves recognizing and understanding emotions, maintaining composure, and responding appropriately. Emotional regulation enhances communication by preventing emotional outbursts and promoting rational decision-making.

8. Cultural Awareness

CULTURAL AWARENESS is the recognition and appreciation of cultural differences and similarities. It involves understanding and respecting diverse cultural norms, values, and communication styles. Cultural awareness promotes effective communication in multicultural settings by fostering inclusivity and reducing misunderstandings.

9. Social Perceptiveness

SOCIAL PERCEPTIVENESS is the ability to observe and interpret social cues, such as body language, facial expressions, and tone of voice. It helps individuals understand others' emotions, intentions, and reactions. Social perceptiveness enhances communication by enabling individuals to respond appropriately and adapt to social dynamics.

How to Develop Active Listening Skills

ACTIVE LISTENING IS a foundational social skill that enhances communication and strengthens relationships. Developing active listening skills involves practicing attentiveness, empathy, and effective response techniques. The following strategies can help individuals become more proficient active listeners.

1. Focus on the Speaker

ACTIVE LISTENING BEGINS with fully focusing on the speaker. This means giving them your undivided attention, avoiding distractions, and being present in the moment. To enhance focus:

- Maintain eye contact with the speaker.

- Minimize external distractions, such as turning off electronic devices or finding a quiet place to talk.

- Avoid interrupting the speaker and allow them to express their thoughts fully.

2. Show Genuine Interest

DEMONSTRATING GENUINE interest in what the speaker is saying fosters trust and encourages open communication. To show interest:

- Use affirmative body language, such as nodding or leaning slightly forward.

- Make verbal acknowledgments, such as "I see," "That's interesting," or "Tell me more."

- Ask open-ended questions that encourage the speaker to elaborate and share more details.

3. Practice Empathy

EMPATHY IS A KEY COMPONENT of active listening. It involves understanding and validating the speaker's emotions and perspective. To practice empathy:

- Reflect on the speaker's emotions and imagine how they might feel.

- Use empathetic statements, such as "That must have been challenging" or "I can understand why you feel that way."

- Avoid judging or offering unsolicited advice; focus on being supportive and understanding.

4. Paraphrase and Summarize

PARAPHRASING AND SUMMARIZING help ensure that you understand the speaker's message accurately and show that you are actively engaged in the conversation. To paraphrase and summarize effectively:

- Restate the speaker's main points in your own words, such as "So, you're saying that..."

- Summarize the key points of the conversation to confirm understanding, such as "To summarize, it sounds like..."

- Check for accuracy by asking the speaker if your summary is correct.

5. Avoid Assumptions and Judgments

ACTIVE LISTENING REQUIRES an open mind and a non-judgmental attitude. Avoid making assumptions or jumping to conclusions about the speaker's message. To avoid assumptions and judgments:

- Listen to the entire message before forming an opinion.

- Be aware of your biases and strive to remain objective.

- Ask clarifying questions if you are unsure about the speaker's meaning.

6. Provide Constructive Feedback

PROVIDING FEEDBACK shows that you are engaged and interested in the conversation. Constructive feedback helps the speaker feel heard and understood. To provide constructive feedback:

- Offer positive reinforcement, such as "I appreciate your perspective" or "That's a great point."

- Share your thoughts and feelings honestly and respectfully.

- Use "I" statements to express your opinions, such as "I think" or "I feel," rather than making generalizations or criticisms.

7. Be Patient and Practice Patience

ACTIVE LISTENING REQUIRES patience and the willingness to let the conversation unfold naturally. Avoid rushing the speaker or finishing their sentences. To practice patience:

- Allow the speaker to take their time and express themselves fully.

- Resist the urge to interrupt or fill in pauses in the conversation.

- Be comfortable with silence, as it gives the speaker time to think and reflect.

8. Reflect on Your Listening Skills

REGULAR SELF-REFLECTION can help you identify areas for improvement in your active listening skills. Consider keeping a listening journal to track your progress and reflect on your experiences. Ask yourself questions such as:

- How well did I focus on the speaker?

- Did I show genuine interest and empathy?

- What could I do differently to improve my listening skills?

Techniques for Improving Verbal and Non-Verbal Communication

EFFECTIVE COMMUNICATION involves both verbal and non-verbal elements. Improving verbal and non-verbal communication skills enhances your ability to convey messages clearly, build rapport, and navigate social interactions successfully. The following techniques can help you develop and refine these skills.

Improving Verbal Communication

1. CLARITY AND CONCISENESS

Clear and concise communication ensures that your message is understood without confusion or ambiguity. To improve clarity and conciseness:

- Organize your thoughts before speaking.

- Use simple and straightforward language.

- Avoid jargon or technical terms unless necessary, and explain them if used.

- Stay on topic and avoid unnecessary digressions.

2. Appropriate Tone and Volume

The tone and volume of your voice convey emotions and attitudes. Using an appropriate tone and volume enhances the effectiveness of your message. To improve tone and volume:

- Match your tone to the context and content of your message (e.g., a respectful tone for serious topics, an enthusiastic tone for positive news).

- Adjust your volume to ensure you are heard without shouting or whispering.

- Practice varying your tone and volume to maintain listener interest and emphasize key points.

3. Active Engagement

Engaging your audience actively fosters a dynamic and interactive conversation. To improve active engagement:

- Ask open-ended questions to encourage dialogue and invite input.

- Use inclusive language, such as "we" or "us," to create a sense of collaboration.

- Acknowledge and build on others' contributions to keep the conversation flowing.

4. Positive Language

Using positive language creates a constructive and supportive communication environment. To improve positive language:

- Focus on what can be done rather than what cannot.

- Use encouraging and affirming words and phrases.

- Avoid negative or critical language that may discourage or alienate others.

5. Storytelling

Storytelling is a powerful tool for engaging listeners and making your message memorable. To improve storytelling:

- Use personal anecdotes or relevant examples to illustrate your points.

- Structure your stories with a clear beginning, middle, and end.

- Include sensory details and emotions to make your stories vivid and relatable.

Improving Non-Verbal Communication

1. EYE CONTACT

Eye contact conveys confidence, interest, and respect. To improve eye contact:

- Maintain eye contact with the speaker or audience while speaking.

- Avoid staring or looking away too frequently, as this can signal discomfort or disinterest.

- Practice making eye contact in various social settings to build confidence.

2. Facial Expressions

Facial expressions communicate emotions and reinforce verbal messages. To improve facial expressions:

- Be aware of your facial expressions and ensure they align with your verbal message.

- Practice expressing different emotions through facial expressions in front of a mirror.

- Observe others' facial expressions and learn to interpret their emotional cues.

3. Body Language

Body language, including posture, gestures, and movement, plays a significant role in communication. To improve body language:

- Adopt an open and relaxed posture, such as standing or sitting up straight with uncrossed arms.

- Use gestures to emphasize key points and convey enthusiasm.

- Avoid fidgeting or nervous movements that may distract from your message.

4. Proxemics (Personal Space)

Proxemics refers to the use of personal space in communication. To improve proxemics:

- Be mindful of cultural norms and personal preferences regarding personal space.

- Respect others' personal space and avoid standing too close or too far away.

- Adjust your distance based on the context and the nature of the interaction.

5. Tone of Voice

The tone of voice conveys emotions and attitudes, complementing the verbal message. To improve the tone of voice:

- Match your tone to the content and context of your message.

- Practice using different tones to convey various emotions, such as warmth, excitement, or seriousness.

- Pay attention to the tone of others' voices and respond appropriately.

6. Active Gestures

Active gestures enhance verbal communication and help convey meaning more effectively. To improve active gestures:

- Use hand movements to emphasize points and illustrate concepts.

- Ensure gestures are natural and not overly exaggerated or distracting.

- Observe skilled communicators and incorporate effective gestures into your own style.

7. Mirroring and Matching

Mirroring and matching involve subtly imitating others' non-verbal cues to build rapport and foster connection. To practice mirroring and matching:

- Observe the other person's body language, facial expressions, and tone of voice.

- Reflect these cues in a subtle and respectful manner to create a sense of alignment and empathy.

- Avoid overdoing it, as excessive mirroring can come across as insincere or manipulative.

8. Self-Awareness

Self-awareness of your non-verbal communication is crucial for improvement. To enhance self-awareness:

- Reflect on your non-verbal behaviors and how they align with your verbal messages.

- Seek feedback from trusted friends or colleagues about your non-verbal communication.

- Record and review your interactions to identify areas for improvement.

Personal Stories and Case Studies

TO ILLUSTRATE THE IMPACT of developing social skills, let's explore some personal stories and case studies.

Case Study 1: Emma's Journey to Effective Communication

EMMA, A 28-YEAR-OLD project manager, struggled with active listening and non-verbal communication. She often found herself interrupting others and failing to pick up on social cues, leading to misunderstandings with her team. Emma decided to work with a communication coach to enhance her social skills.

Through active listening exercises, Emma learned to focus fully on the speaker and show genuine interest. She practiced paraphrasing and summarizing to ensure accurate understanding. Emma also worked on her non-verbal communication by maintaining eye contact, using positive body language, and aligning her facial expressions with her verbal messages.

Over time, Emma's communication skills improved significantly. Her team noticed that she became a better listener and more empathetic communicator. Emma's ability to resolve conflicts and foster collaboration enhanced her effectiveness as a project manager and strengthened her relationships with colleagues.

Case Study 2: David's Transformation through Verbal and Non-Verbal Techniques

DAVID, A 35-YEAR-OLD sales executive, faced challenges with verbal and non-verbal communication. He often struggled to articulate his ideas clearly and found it difficult to connect with clients. David decided to attend a communication skills workshop to address these issues.

During the workshop, David learned techniques for improving clarity and conciseness in his verbal communication. He practiced organizing his thoughts, using positive language, and engaging his audience through storytelling. David also focused on enhancing his non-verbal communication by maintaining eye contact, using gestures effectively, and adopting an open posture.

David's transformation was remarkable. He became more confident in his ability to communicate with clients and colleagues. His improved verbal and non-verbal skills led to better client relationships, increased sales, and greater professional success.

Personal Story: Sarah's Path to Assertiveness and Empathy

SARAH, A 30-YEAR-OLD teacher, struggled with assertiveness and empathy in her interactions with students and colleagues. She often found it difficult to express her needs and opinions and felt overwhelmed by others' emotions. Sarah decided to seek guidance from a mentor to develop these social skills.

Through role-playing and feedback, Sarah practiced assertiveness by expressing her thoughts clearly and setting boundaries. She also worked on enhancing her empathy by actively listening to her students, validating their emotions, and responding with compassion.

Sarah's path to assertiveness and empathy led to significant improvements in her teaching and relationships. She became more confident in managing classroom dynamics, resolving conflicts, and supporting her students' emotional needs. Sarah's empathetic approach fostered a positive and inclusive learning environment.

Conclusion

Developing social skills is essential for effective communication, building strong relationships, and navigating social interactions with confidence. By focusing on core social skills such as active listening, verbal communication, non-verbal communication, empathy, assertiveness, conflict resolution, emotional regulation, cultural awareness, and social perceptiveness, individuals can enhance their ability to connect with others meaningfully.

Personal stories and case studies demonstrate that transformation is possible with practice, self-reflection, and a commitment to growth. As you continue reading this book, remember that developing social skills is an ongoing journey that requires patience, perseverance, and self-compassion. By embracing this journey and applying the insights and techniques discussed, you can develop the social confidence needed to thrive in both personal and professional settings. Let's move forward together, step by step, towards a more skilled, confident, and socially adept you.

Chapter 5: Overcoming Social Anxiety

Understanding Social Anxiety and Its Symptoms

Social anxiety, also known as social anxiety disorder (SAD), is a pervasive fear of social situations where one might be scrutinized, judged, or humiliated by others. This fear goes beyond typical nervousness or shyness; it can be debilitating, affecting various aspects of life, from personal relationships to professional opportunities.

Social anxiety often begins in adolescence and can persist into adulthood if not addressed. It is characterized by an intense fear of negative evaluation, leading individuals to avoid social interactions or endure them with significant distress. Understanding the symptoms and underlying causes of social anxiety is crucial for developing effective strategies to manage and overcome it.

Symptoms of Social Anxiety

SOCIAL ANXIETY MANIFESTS in various physical, emotional, and behavioral symptoms. Recognizing these symptoms is the first step toward addressing and managing the disorder.

Physical Symptoms:

- SWEATING: EXCESSIVE sweating, particularly in social situations, is a common symptom of social anxiety.

- Trembling or Shaking: Individuals may experience noticeable trembling or shaking, especially in the hands.

- Heart Palpitations: Rapid or irregular heartbeats can occur in anticipation of or during social interactions.

- Dry Mouth: Anxiety can lead to a dry mouth, making it difficult to speak comfortably.

- Muscle Tension: Social anxiety often results in tense muscles, leading to discomfort or pain.

- Dizziness or Lightheadedness: Feeling dizzy or lightheaded is a common physical reaction to anxiety.

- Nausea: Some individuals may experience nausea or gastrointestinal distress in social situations.

Emotional Symptoms:

- INTENSE FEAR: A PERVASIVE fear of being judged, criticized, or humiliated in social settings.

- Excessive Worry: Persistent worry about upcoming social interactions or past social experiences.

- Self-Consciousness: Heightened self-awareness and preoccupation with how one is perceived by others.

- Embarrassment: Frequent feelings of embarrassment or shame in social contexts.

- Low Self-Esteem: Negative self-perception and a lack of confidence in social abilities.

Behavioral Symptoms:

- AVOIDANCE: ACTIVELY avoiding social situations, such as parties, meetings, or public speaking.

- Escape Behaviors: Leaving social events early or finding excuses to avoid participation.

- Overpreparation: Excessive preparation for social interactions to avoid perceived failure or embarrassment.

- Safety Behaviors: Engaging in behaviors that reduce anxiety temporarily, such as avoiding eye contact or speaking softly.

- Isolation: Withdrawing from social activities and relationships, leading to loneliness and depression.

Causes of Social Anxiety

THE DEVELOPMENT OF social anxiety is influenced by a combination of genetic, environmental, and psychological factors. Understanding these causes can provide insight into the disorder and inform effective treatment approaches.

Genetic Factors:

- FAMILY HISTORY: SOCIAL anxiety can run in families, suggesting a genetic predisposition to the disorder. Individuals with a family history of anxiety or mood disorders are at a higher risk of developing social anxiety.

- Temperament: Children with a shy or inhibited temperament are more likely to develop social anxiety. This temperament is often characterized by heightened sensitivity to new or unfamiliar situations.

Environmental Factors:

- EARLY EXPERIENCES: Negative social experiences, such as bullying, teasing, or criticism, can contribute to the development of social anxiety. Traumatic events or adverse childhood experiences can also play a role.

- Parenting Styles: Overprotective, critical, or controlling parenting can foster social anxiety. Children may internalize these behaviors, leading to a fear of judgment or rejection.

- Social Learning: Observing and modeling anxious behaviors from parents or peers can contribute to the development of social anxiety.

Psychological Factors:

- COGNITIVE DISTORTIONS: Negative thought patterns, such as catastrophizing or overgeneralizing, can exacerbate social anxiety. Individuals may perceive social interactions as more threatening than they are.

- Low Self-Esteem: A negative self-concept and lack of confidence can fuel social anxiety. Individuals with low self-esteem may believe they are inadequate or unworthy of positive social interactions.

- Perfectionism: A desire to meet unrealistic standards or avoid making mistakes can lead to excessive fear of failure or criticism in social settings.

Practical Strategies for Managing and Reducing Social Anxiety

MANAGING SOCIAL ANXIETY involves a combination of practical strategies and therapeutic techniques. The following approaches can help individuals reduce anxiety, build confidence, and improve their social interactions.

1. Gradual Exposure

GRADUAL EXPOSURE INVOLVES facing feared social situations in a systematic and controlled manner. This approach helps individuals build confidence and reduce anxiety over time. To practice gradual exposure:

- Create a Hierarchy: List social situations that trigger anxiety, ranking them from least to most anxiety-provoking.

- Start Small: Begin with situations that cause mild anxiety and gradually work up to more challenging scenarios.

- Practice Regularly: Engage in exposure exercises consistently to build familiarity and reduce fear.

- Reflect on Progress: After each exposure, reflect on the experience and any progress made. Acknowledge successes and identify areas for improvement.

2. Deep Breathing and Relaxation Techniques

DEEP BREATHING AND relaxation techniques can help manage the physical symptoms of anxiety. These practices promote a state of calm and reduce the body's stress response. To practice deep breathing:

- Find a Quiet Space: Sit or lie down in a comfortable position in a quiet environment.

- Breathe Slowly: Inhale deeply through your nose for a count of four, hold for a count of four, and exhale slowly through your mouth for a count of six.

- Repeat: Continue this pattern for several minutes, focusing on the sensation of your breath.

Other relaxation techniques, such as progressive muscle relaxation and visualization, can also be effective in managing anxiety.

3. Cognitive Restructuring

COGNITIVE RESTRUCTURING involves identifying and challenging negative thought patterns that contribute to social anxiety. This technique helps individuals develop more realistic and positive perspectives. To practice cognitive restructuring:

- Identify Negative Thoughts: Pay attention to negative thoughts that arise in social situations, such as "Everyone will judge me" or "I always make a fool of myself."

- Examine Evidence: Evaluate the evidence for and against these thoughts. Consider past experiences and whether the thoughts are based on facts or assumptions.

- Challenge Distortions: Identify cognitive distortions, such as catastrophizing or mind-reading, and challenge their validity.

- Reframe Thoughts: Replace negative thoughts with more balanced and realistic ones, such as "It's okay to make mistakes" or "People are generally understanding and supportive."

4. Social Skills Training

SOCIAL SKILLS TRAINING involves learning and practicing specific behaviors to improve social interactions. This training can enhance confidence and reduce anxiety in social settings. Key components of social skills training include:

- Role-Playing: Practice social interactions through role-playing exercises with a therapist or trusted friend.

- Feedback and Reinforcement: Receive constructive feedback and positive reinforcement to build confidence.

- Modeling: Observe and imitate effective social behaviors demonstrated by others.

5. Mindfulness and Acceptance

MINDFULNESS AND ACCEPTANCE practices help individuals manage anxiety by focusing on the present moment and accepting their experiences without judgment. These practices promote emotional regulation and reduce reactivity to anxiety triggers. To practice mindfulness:

- Mindfulness Meditation: Engage in regular mindfulness meditation, focusing on the breath, body sensations, or a specific point of attention.

- Acceptance and Commitment Therapy (ACT): Use ACT techniques to accept anxious thoughts and feelings without attempting to change them. Focus on committed actions aligned with personal values.

6. Building Self-Esteem

IMPROVING SELF-ESTEEM can reduce social anxiety by fostering a more positive self-view and increasing confidence in social interactions. Strategies for building self-esteem include:

- Positive Affirmations: Use positive affirmations to counteract negative self-talk and reinforce a positive self-concept.

- Setting and Achieving Goals: Set realistic and achievable goals to build a sense of accomplishment and competence.

- Recognizing Strengths: Identify and celebrate personal strengths and achievements, no matter how small.

7. Seeking Professional Help

FOR INDIVIDUALS WITH severe social anxiety, seeking professional help from a therapist or counselor can be highly beneficial. Therapeutic approaches, such as cognitive-behavioral therapy (CBT), acceptance and commitment therapy (ACT), and exposure therapy, are effective in treating social anxiety. Medication may also be prescribed in some cases to manage symptoms.

Cognitive-Behavioral Techniques for Challenging Negative Thoughts

COGNITIVE-BEHAVIORAL therapy (CBT) is a widely used and effective treatment for social anxiety. CBT focuses on identifying and challenging negative thought patterns and behaviors that contribute to anxiety. The following cognitive-behavioral techniques can help individuals reframe negative thoughts and develop healthier perspectives.

1. Cognitive Restructuring

COGNITIVE RESTRUCTURING involves identifying and challenging irrational or distorted thoughts that contribute to anxiety. This technique helps individuals develop more balanced and realistic perspectives. The steps for cognitive restructuring include:

Step 1: Identify Negative Thoughts

THE FIRST STEP IN COGNITIVE restructuring is to identify negative thoughts that arise in social situations. These thoughts often reflect cognitive distortions, such as:

- Catastrophizing: Expecting the worst possible outcome (e.g., "Everyone will think I'm an idiot").

- Mind-Reading: Assuming you know what others are thinking (e.g., "They must think I'm boring").

- Overgeneralizing: Making broad conclusions based on a single event (e.g., "I always mess up in social situations").

Step 2: Examine Evidence

EVALUATE THE EVIDENCE for and against these negative thoughts. Consider past experiences and whether the thoughts are based on facts or assumptions. Ask yourself questions such as:

- What evidence supports this thought?

- What evidence contradicts this thought?

- Have I had similar thoughts before, and were they accurate?

Step 3: Challenge Distortions

IDENTIFY COGNITIVE distortions in your negative thoughts and challenge their validity. For example:

- Catastrophizing: Consider whether the worst-case scenario is likely and whether it would be as catastrophic as you imagine.

- Mind-Reading: Acknowledge that you cannot read others' minds and that their thoughts may be different from what you assume.

- Overgeneralizing: Recognize that one negative experience does not define all social interactions.

Step 4: Reframe Thoughts

REPLACE NEGATIVE THOUGHTS with more balanced and realistic ones. For example:

- Negative Thought: "Everyone will judge me if I speak up in the meeting."

- Reframed Thought: "It's normal to feel nervous, but people are likely focused on their own concerns. Speaking up can show my perspective and contribute to the discussion."

2. Behavioral Experiments

BEHAVIORAL EXPERIMENTS involve testing the validity of negative thoughts and beliefs through real-life experiences. This technique helps individuals gather evidence to challenge their anxieties and develop more accurate perspectives. The steps for conducting behavioral experiments include:

Step 1: Identify a Negative Thought or Belief

CHOOSE A SPECIFIC NEGATIVE thought or belief to test. For example:

- Negative Thought: "If I start a conversation with a stranger, they will think I'm awkward and reject me."

Step 2: Design an Experiment

PLAN A SPECIFIC ACTION to test the negative thought or belief. For example:

- Experiment: "I will start a conversation with a stranger at the coffee shop and observe their reaction."

Step 3: Predict the Outcome

PREDICT WHAT YOU THINK will happen during the experiment based on your negative thought or belief. For example:

- Prediction: "The stranger will think I'm awkward and will want to end the conversation quickly."

Step 4: Conduct the Experiment

CARRY OUT THE PLANNED action and observe the actual outcome. Pay attention to the details and note any differences from your prediction.

Step 5: Reflect on the Results

COMPARE THE PREDICTED outcome with the actual outcome. Reflect on any discrepancies and what you learned from the experiment. For example:

- Actual Outcome: "The stranger was friendly and engaged in the conversation. They didn't seem to think I was awkward."

- Reflection: "My prediction was not accurate. This experience challenges my belief that others will reject me if I start a conversation."

3. Thought Records

THOUGHT RECORDS ARE a structured way to track and analyze negative thoughts, identify cognitive distortions, and reframe them with more balanced perspectives. The steps for completing a thought record include:

Step 1: Describe the Situation

WRITE DOWN THE SPECIFIC situation that triggered your anxiety. Include details about the context, people involved, and any relevant circumstances.

Step 2: Identify Emotions

IDENTIFY AND RATE THE intensity of your emotions in response to the situation. For example:

- Emotion: Anxiety

- Intensity: 8 out of 10

Step 3: Record Negative Thoughts

WRITE DOWN THE AUTOMATIC negative thoughts that arose in response to the situation. Include any cognitive distortions you notice.

Step 4: Examine Evidence

EVALUATE THE EVIDENCE for and against your negative thoughts. Consider past experiences and any objective information.

Step 5: Challenge and Reframe Thoughts

CHALLENGE THE VALIDITY of your negative thoughts and reframe them with more balanced and realistic perspectives. For example:

- Negative Thought: "I'll embarrass myself if I speak up in the meeting."

- Evidence For: "I felt nervous and stumbled over my words last time."

- Evidence Against: "I've spoken up in meetings before without any major issues. People seemed to appreciate my input."

- Reframed Thought: "It's normal to feel nervous, but I have valuable insights to share. It's worth speaking up."

Step 6: Reflect on Emotions

RE-RATE THE INTENSITY of your emotions after reframing your thoughts. Note any changes and reflect on how the exercise influenced your perspective.

4. Coping Statements

COPING STATEMENTS ARE positive affirmations or reminders that help individuals manage anxiety in challenging situations. These statements provide reassurance and promote a more constructive mindset. Examples of coping statements include:

- "It's okay to feel anxious; I can handle this."

- "I don't have to be perfect; doing my best is enough."

- "People are generally understanding and supportive."

- "I can take things one step at a time."

Incorporate coping statements into your daily routine and use them as needed in anxiety-provoking situations.

5. Problem-Solving Skills

EFFECTIVE PROBLEM-SOLVING skills can reduce anxiety by providing a structured approach to addressing challenges and making decisions. The steps for problem-solving include:

Step 1: Define the Problem

CLEARLY DEFINE THE problem you are facing. Be specific about the nature of the issue and any relevant details.

Step 2: Generate Solutions

BRAINSTORM POTENTIAL solutions to the problem. Consider a range of options, including those that may seem less obvious.

Step 3: Evaluate Options

EVALUATE THE PROS AND cons of each potential solution. Consider factors such as feasibility, potential outcomes, and any associated risks.

Step 4: Choose a Solution

SELECT THE MOST VIABLE and effective solution based on your evaluation. Consider any necessary steps or resources required to implement the solution.

Step 5: Implement the Solution

TAKE ACTION TO IMPLEMENT the chosen solution. Follow through with the necessary steps and monitor progress.

Step 6: Review and Reflect

REVIEW THE OUTCOME of the implemented solution. Reflect on what worked well and any areas for improvement. Use this information to refine your problem-solving approach in the future.

6. Building Resilience

BUILDING RESILIENCE involves developing the capacity to adapt and recover from challenges and setbacks. Resilience helps individuals maintain a positive outlook and manage anxiety more effectively. Strategies for building resilience include:

Cultivating a Growth Mindset

ADOPTING A GROWTH MINDSET involves viewing challenges as opportunities for learning and growth. This perspective promotes resilience by encouraging individuals to embrace difficulties and persist in the face of obstacles.

Developing Healthy Coping Mechanisms

HEALTHY COPING MECHANISMS, such as exercise, meditation, and creative activities, provide constructive outlets for managing stress and anxiety.

Incorporating these activities into daily routines enhances overall well-being and resilience.

Seeking Social Support

BUILDING AND MAINTAINING a strong support network provides emotional and practical support during challenging times. Connecting with friends, family, or support groups fosters resilience by promoting a sense of belonging and shared understanding.

Practicing Self-Compassion

SELF-COMPASSION INVOLVES treating oneself with kindness and understanding, especially during difficult times. Practicing self-compassion enhances resilience by reducing self-criticism and promoting emotional well-being.

Personal Stories and Case Studies

TO ILLUSTRATE THE IMPACT of overcoming social anxiety, let's explore some personal stories and case studies.

Case Study 1: John's Journey to Overcoming Social Anxiety

JOHN, A 32-YEAR-OLD software engineer, struggled with severe social anxiety. He avoided social gatherings, meetings, and public speaking opportunities, fearing judgment and rejection. John's anxiety affected his career growth and personal relationships.

John decided to seek help from a therapist specializing in cognitive-behavioral therapy (CBT). Through CBT, John learned to identify and challenge his negative thoughts. He practiced gradual exposure by attending small social events and gradually increasing the complexity of social interactions.

John also incorporated relaxation techniques, such as deep breathing and mindfulness meditation, into his routine. Over time, John's confidence grew, and his anxiety decreased. He started participating more actively in meetings, building stronger relationships with colleagues, and enjoying social events without overwhelming fear.

Case Study 2: Emily's Transformation through Cognitive Restructuring

EMILY, A 28-YEAR-OLD graphic designer, experienced intense social anxiety, particularly in professional settings. She often worried about making mistakes and being judged by her peers. Emily's anxiety led to avoidance behaviors and hindered her career progress.

Emily's therapist introduced her to cognitive restructuring techniques. She learned to identify and challenge her negative thoughts, replacing them with more balanced perspectives. Emily also practiced behavioral experiments, testing her fears in real-life situations.

With consistent practice, Emily's anxiety diminished. She became more confident in her abilities and started taking on leadership roles in projects. Emily's improved social confidence enhanced her professional success and personal well-being.

Personal Story: Sarah's Path to Building Resilience and Self-Esteem

SARAH, A 25-YEAR-OLD college student, struggled with social anxiety and low self-esteem. She avoided participating in class discussions and social events, fearing judgment and rejection. Sarah's anxiety affected her academic performance and social life.

Determined to overcome her anxiety, Sarah joined a support group on campus. Through the group, she practiced social skills, received feedback, and built a supportive network. Sarah also worked on building her self-esteem by setting and achieving small goals and recognizing her strengths.

Sarah's path to building resilience and self-esteem led to significant improvements. She became more confident in social interactions, participated actively in class, and formed meaningful friendships. Sarah's journey to overcoming social anxiety enriched her college experience and set her on a path to success.

Conclusion

Overcoming social anxiety is a journey that requires patience, perseverance, and a commitment to growth. By understanding the symptoms and underlying causes of social anxiety and implementing practical strategies and cognitive-behavioral techniques, individuals can reduce anxiety, build confidence, and improve their social interactions.

Personal stories and case studies demonstrate that transformation is possible with the right support and approach. As you continue reading this book, remember that overcoming social anxiety is an ongoing process that involves self-compassion, practice, and resilience. By embracing this journey and applying the insights and techniques discussed, you can develop the social confidence needed to thrive in both personal and

Chapter 6: Building Self-Confidence

The Role of Self-Confidence in Social Interactions

Self-confidence is a crucial component of effective social interactions. It influences how we perceive ourselves, how we interact with others, and how others perceive us. Confidence allows us to engage in conversations, express our opinions, and build meaningful relationships without the constant fear of judgment or rejection.

Understanding Self-Confidence

SELF-CONFIDENCE IS the belief in one's abilities, qualities, and judgment. It is a sense of assurance that you can handle various situations and challenges. This assurance comes from a realistic understanding of your strengths and weaknesses and a positive self-perception. Self-confidence is not about being perfect; it's about trusting yourself and your capacity to grow and adapt.

Impact of Self-Confidence on Social Interactions

1. IMPROVED COMMUNICATION

Confident individuals are more likely to engage in conversations, express their thoughts clearly, and listen actively. They are less likely to be hindered by self-doubt or fear of judgment, allowing them to communicate more effectively.

2. Positive Body Language

Self-confidence is often reflected in non-verbal cues such as posture, eye contact, and facial expressions. Confident people tend to have open and relaxed body language, which makes them more approachable and trustworthy.

3. Enhanced Relationship Building

Confidence allows individuals to initiate and maintain relationships more easily. It helps in overcoming social barriers, making it easier to connect with others and build rapport.

4. Greater Resilience

Confident individuals are more resilient to social setbacks and criticism. They are better equipped to handle rejection and bounce back from negative experiences, maintaining their self-esteem and social competence.

5. Increased Opportunities

In both personal and professional contexts, self-confidence opens doors to new opportunities. Confident individuals are more likely to take risks, seek out new experiences, and pursue goals that require social engagement.

The Relationship Between Self-Confidence and Social Anxiety

SELF-CONFIDENCE AND social anxiety are often inversely related. Low self-confidence can contribute to social anxiety, while social anxiety can further erode self-confidence. Building self-confidence can help mitigate social anxiety by fostering a more positive self-view and reducing fear of social judgment.

Exercises and Activities to Boost Self-Confidence

BUILDING SELF-CONFIDENCE is a gradual process that involves self-reflection, skill development, and positive reinforcement. The following exercises and activities can help boost self-confidence and enhance social interactions.

1. Positive Affirmations

Positive affirmations are statements that reinforce self-belief and counteract negative self-talk. Regularly repeating affirmations can help shift your mindset and build confidence. Examples of positive affirmations include:

- "I am capable and confident in my abilities."

- "I deserve love, respect, and happiness."

- "I learn and grow from my experiences."

- "I am proud of who I am and what I can achieve."

To practice positive affirmations, write down a list of affirmations that resonate with you and repeat them daily, preferably in front of a mirror.

2. Visualization

Visualization involves imagining yourself successfully navigating social interactions and achieving your goals. This technique can help reduce anxiety and build confidence by creating a mental image of positive outcomes. To practice visualization:

- Find a quiet and comfortable place to sit or lie down.

- Close your eyes and take a few deep breaths to relax.

- Visualize yourself in a specific social situation, such as giving a presentation or attending a social event.

- Imagine yourself feeling confident, calm, and capable. Focus on the details, such as your body language, tone of voice, and the reactions of others.

- Repeat this exercise regularly to reinforce positive mental imagery.

3. Journaling

Journaling is a powerful tool for self-reflection and self-discovery. It allows you to explore your thoughts, emotions, and experiences, gaining insight into your strengths and areas for growth. To practice journaling:

- Set aside time each day or week to write in a journal.

- Reflect on your social interactions, noting what went well and what could be improved.

- Write about your achievements, challenges, and goals.

- Use journaling prompts to explore specific topics, such as "What makes me feel confident?" or "How can I handle social anxiety?"

4. Setting and Achieving Small Goals

Setting and achieving small, manageable goals can build self-confidence by providing a sense of accomplishment and progress. Start with goals that are realistic and achievable, gradually increasing the difficulty as your confidence grows. Examples of small goals include:

- Introducing yourself to a new colleague.

- Participating in a group discussion.

- Making small talk with a stranger.

- Attending a social event or networking function.

Celebrate your achievements, no matter how small, and use them as stepping stones to tackle more challenging goals.

5. Social Skills Training

Social skills training involves learning and practicing specific behaviors to improve social interactions. This training can enhance confidence by providing the tools and techniques needed to navigate social situations effectively. Key components of social skills training include:

- Role-Playing: Practice social interactions through role-playing exercises with a friend or therapist.

- Feedback and Reinforcement: Receive constructive feedback and positive reinforcement to build confidence.

- Modeling: Observe and imitate effective social behaviors demonstrated by others.

6. Self-Compassion Practices

Self-compassion involves treating yourself with kindness and understanding, especially during difficult times. Practicing self-compassion can reduce self-criticism and foster a more positive self-view. To practice self-compassion:

- Recognize that everyone makes mistakes and experiences setbacks.

- Offer yourself words of comfort and encouragement, such as "It's okay to feel anxious" or "I'm doing my best."

- Engage in self-care activities that nurture your physical, emotional, and mental well-being.

7. Public Speaking Practice

Public speaking can be a significant confidence booster, as it challenges you to communicate effectively in front of an audience. To practice public speaking:

- Join a public speaking group or club, such as Toastmasters.

- Practice giving speeches or presentations in front of friends or family.

- Record yourself speaking and review the footage to identify areas for improvement.

- Focus on improving your posture, eye contact, and vocal delivery.

8. Mindfulness Meditation

Mindfulness meditation helps you stay present and aware of your thoughts and emotions without judgment. This practice can reduce anxiety and promote a sense of calm and confidence. To practice mindfulness meditation:

- Find a quiet and comfortable place to sit.

- Close your eyes and take a few deep breaths to relax.

- Focus on your breath, noticing the sensation of each inhale and exhale.

- When your mind wanders, gently bring your attention back to your breath.

- Practice mindfulness meditation regularly to build awareness and emotional regulation.

9. Volunteering and Helping Others

Volunteering and helping others can boost self-confidence by providing a sense of purpose and fulfillment. Engaging in acts of kindness and service allows you to connect with others and make a positive impact. To get involved in volunteering:

- Find local organizations or causes that align with your interests and values.

- Participate in community service projects or events.

- Offer your skills and expertise to support others in need.

10. Physical Exercise

Physical exercise has numerous benefits for mental health and self-confidence. Regular exercise can improve mood, reduce anxiety, and enhance overall well-being. To incorporate exercise into your routine:

- Choose activities that you enjoy, such as walking, running, swimming, or dancing.

- Set realistic fitness goals and track your progress.

- Join a fitness class or group to stay motivated and connect with others.

Setting and Achieving Personal Goals for Social Growth

SETTING AND ACHIEVING personal goals is a powerful way to build self-confidence and foster social growth. Goals provide direction, motivation, and a sense of purpose, helping you make meaningful progress in your social interactions. The following steps can guide you in setting and achieving personal goals for social growth.

1. Identify Your Goals

Begin by identifying specific goals that align with your values, interests, and aspirations. Consider areas where you want to improve or challenges you want to overcome. Examples of social growth goals include:

- Improving your public speaking skills.

- Expanding your social network and making new friends.

- Enhancing your ability to handle social anxiety.

- Building stronger relationships with colleagues or family members.

2. Make Your Goals SMART

To increase the likelihood of achieving your goals, make them SMART: Specific, Measurable, Achievable, Relevant, and Time-bound. A SMART goal provides clear criteria for success and helps you stay focused and motivated. For example:

- Specific: Clearly define what you want to achieve (e.g., "I want to improve my public speaking skills").

- Measurable: Establish criteria to measure your progress (e.g., "I will give three presentations over the next three months").

- Achievable: Ensure your goal is realistic and attainable (e.g., "I will practice speaking in front of friends and family").

- Relevant: Make sure your goal aligns with your values and long-term objectives (e.g., "Improving public speaking will enhance my career prospects").

- Time-bound: Set a deadline for achieving your goal (e.g., "I will achieve this goal by the end of the year").

3. Break Down Your Goals

Large goals can feel overwhelming, so it's important to break them down into smaller, manageable steps. This approach allows you to make steady progress and maintain motivation. For example, if your goal is to improve your public speaking skills, you might break it down into the following steps:

- Research and join a public speaking group or club.

- Attend meetings and observe experienced speakers.

- Practice speaking in front of a mirror or recording yourself.

- Give a short speech in front of friends or family.

- Gradually increase the length and complexity of your speeches.

4. Create an Action Plan

Develop a detailed action plan outlining the specific steps you will take to achieve your goals. Include timelines, resources, and any support you may need. An action plan provides a clear roadmap and helps you stay organized and focused. For example:

- Week 1: Research public speaking groups and clubs in your area.

- Week 2: Attend your first meeting and introduce yourself.

- Week 3: Practice a short speech in front of a mirror or record yourself.

- Week 4: Give your first speech in front of friends or family.

- Ongoing: Attend meetings regularly, participate in speaking opportunities, and seek feedback.

5. Monitor Your Progress

Regularly monitor your progress toward achieving your goals. Track your achievements, reflect on your experiences, and identify any challenges or obstacles. Monitoring your progress allows you to make adjustments as needed and stay motivated. Consider keeping a journal or using a goal-tracking app to document your journey.

6. Celebrate Your Achievements

Celebrate your achievements, no matter how small, to reinforce positive behaviors and build confidence. Acknowledging your successes boosts motivation and provides a sense of accomplishment. Celebrate milestones along the way and reward yourself for your hard work and dedication.

7. Seek Support and Accountability

Seeking support and accountability can enhance your efforts to achieve your goals. Share your goals with friends, family, or a mentor who can provide encouragement, feedback, and guidance. Consider joining a support group or finding an accountability partner to help you stay on track and motivated.

8. Stay Flexible and Adaptable

Stay flexible and adaptable in your approach to achieving your goals. Life is unpredictable, and you may encounter obstacles or setbacks along the way. Be open to adjusting your action plan and timelines as needed. Remember that progress is not always linear, and setbacks are a natural part of the growth process.

9. Reflect on Your Growth

Take time to reflect on your growth and the lessons you've learned throughout your journey. Reflecting on your experiences helps you gain insight into your strengths, areas for improvement, and the strategies that worked best for you. Use this reflection to inform your future goals and continue your personal development.

10. Set New Goals

As you achieve your initial goals, set new ones to maintain momentum and continue your social growth. Setting new goals keeps you motivated and focused on your ongoing development. Each goal you achieve builds your confidence and prepares you for more significant challenges and opportunities.

Personal Stories and Case Studies

TO ILLUSTRATE THE IMPACT of building self-confidence, let's explore some personal stories and case studies.

Case Study 1: Maria's Journey to Building Self-Confidence

MARIA, A 29-YEAR-OLD marketing professional, struggled with low self-confidence and social anxiety. She often avoided networking events and public speaking opportunities, fearing judgment and rejection. Maria decided to work with a life coach to enhance her self-confidence and improve her social interactions.

Through regular coaching sessions, Maria learned to identify and challenge her negative thoughts. She practiced positive affirmations and visualization exercises to build her self-belief. Maria also set small, achievable goals, such as introducing herself to new colleagues and participating in team meetings.

Over time, Maria's confidence grew. She became more comfortable in social settings and started attending networking events. Her improved self-confidence led to new career opportunities, stronger professional relationships, and a more fulfilling social life.

Case Study 2: James's Transformation through Public Speaking

JAMES, A 35-YEAR-OLD software engineer, faced challenges with public speaking and self-confidence. He often felt anxious and self-conscious when presenting his ideas in meetings. James decided to join a public speaking club to improve his communication skills and build confidence.

At the club, James participated in regular speaking exercises and received constructive feedback from fellow members. He practiced giving speeches on various topics, gradually increasing his comfort level and confidence. James also worked on his non-verbal communication, such as maintaining eye contact and using gestures effectively.

James's transformation was remarkable. He became more confident in his public speaking abilities and started taking on leadership roles in his team. His improved self-confidence enhanced his professional success and personal well-being.

Personal Story: Emily's Path to Self-Compassion and Social Growth

EMILY, A 27-YEAR-OLD teacher, struggled with self-doubt and low self-esteem. She often felt inadequate in her teaching role and avoided social interactions with colleagues. Emily decided to seek guidance from a therapist to build her self-confidence and improve her social skills.

Through therapy, Emily learned to practice self-compassion and challenge her negative self-talk. She engaged in self-care activities and set small, achievable goals for social growth. Emily also joined a support group for teachers, where she practiced social skills and received encouragement from peers.

Emily's path to self-compassion and social growth led to significant improvements. She became more confident in her teaching abilities and started building stronger relationships with colleagues. Emily's journey to building self-confidence enriched her professional and personal life.

CONCLUSION

Building self-confidence is essential for effective social interactions, personal growth, and overall well-being. By understanding the role of self-confidence in social interactions and implementing exercises and activities to boost confidence, individuals can enhance their social competence and navigate social situations with assurance.

Personal stories and case studies demonstrate that transformation is possible with the right strategies and mindset. Setting and achieving personal goals for social growth provides direction, motivation, and a sense of purpose, helping individuals make meaningful progress in their social interactions.

As you continue reading this book, remember that building self-confidence is an ongoing journey that requires patience, practice, and self-compassion. By embracing this journey and applying the insights and techniques discussed, you can develop the self-confidence needed to thrive in both personal and professional settings. Let's move forward together, step by step, towards a more confident, empowered, and socially adept you.

Chapter 7: Effective Conversation Techniques

How to Start and Sustain Conversations

Effective conversations are the cornerstone of building relationships, both personally and professionally. They require a blend of confidence, skill, and sensitivity to navigate the complexities of human interaction. This chapter explores various techniques for starting and sustaining conversations, the art of asking questions and showing interest, and tips for making meaningful connections through dialogue.

1. Overcoming Initial Hesitation

STARTING A CONVERSATION can be intimidating, especially in unfamiliar settings. Overcoming initial hesitation involves building confidence and using strategies that make initiating conversations easier.

Mindset Shift

ADOPTING A POSITIVE mindset is crucial. View conversations as opportunities to learn and connect rather than fearing judgment or rejection. Remind yourself that most people appreciate friendly interactions and are likely to respond positively.

Body Language

OPEN AND APPROACHABLE body language can signal your readiness to engage in conversation. Maintain good posture, make eye contact, and offer a genuine smile. These non-verbal cues can make others feel more comfortable approaching you.

Ice Breakers

HAVING A FEW ICE BREAKERS ready can help initiate conversations smoothly. Ice breakers can be context-specific, such as commenting on a shared experience or asking about the event you're attending. Examples include:

- "Hi, I'm [Your Name]. How do you know the host?"

- "This place has an amazing atmosphere. Have you been here before?"

- "I couldn't help but notice your book. Are you a fan of [author/genre]?"

2. Establishing Common Ground

FINDING COMMON GROUND is a powerful way to connect with others and sustain conversations. It involves identifying shared interests, experiences, or opinions that can serve as conversation starters.

Observation

Observe your surroundings and the person you wish to engage with. Look for clues such as what they're wearing, reading, or discussing with others. These observations can provide a natural segue into a conversation.

Compliments

Genuine compliments can create a positive atmosphere and make the other person feel valued. Compliment something specific, such as their outfit, a piece of jewelry, or their knowledge on a topic. Ensure your compliment is sincere and appropriate.

Shared Experiences

REFERRING TO SHARED experiences, such as being at the same event, living in the same city, or working in the same industry, can provide a solid foundation for conversation. Shared experiences create a sense of connection and make the conversation flow more naturally.

3. Active Listening and Engagement

ACTIVE LISTENING IS essential for sustaining conversations. It involves fully engaging with the speaker, showing empathy, and responding thoughtfully.

Focus on the Speaker

GIVE THE SPEAKER YOUR full attention. Avoid distractions, such as checking your phone or looking around the room. Maintain eye contact and use affirmative body language to show that you are listening.

Reflect and Paraphrase

REFLECTING AND PARAPHRASING what the speaker has said demonstrates that you are engaged and understanding their message. This technique encourages the speaker to elaborate and keeps the conversation flowing. For example:

- Speaker: "I've been really busy at work lately."

- You: "It sounds like your workload has increased. How are you managing everything?"

Empathetic Responses

SHOW EMPATHY BY ACKNOWLEDGING the speaker's emotions and experiences. Use empathetic statements such as, "That sounds challenging," or "I can see why you feel that way." Empathy fosters a deeper connection and encourages open communication.

4. Balancing Speaking and Listening

A BALANCED CONVERSATION involves both speaking and listening. Aim to contribute to the conversation without dominating it and give the other person space to share their thoughts and experiences.

Turn-Taking

PRACTICE TURN-TAKING by allowing the other person to speak and then responding thoughtfully. Avoid interrupting or monopolizing the conversation. Use verbal and non-verbal cues, such as nodding or pausing, to signal that it's their turn to speak.

Sharing Personal Stories

SHARING PERSONAL STORIES can make the conversation more engaging and relatable. Ensure your stories are relevant to the topic and concise. Sharing too much or going off on tangents can overwhelm the other person.

Open-Ended Questions

ASK OPEN-ENDED QUESTIONS that encourage the other person to share more about themselves. Open-ended questions cannot be answered with a simple "yes" or "no" and often lead to more meaningful dialogue. Examples include:

- "What do you enjoy most about your job?"

- "How did you get interested in [hobby/interest]?"

- "What are some of your favorite places to visit?"

The Art of Asking Questions and Showing Interest

ASKING QUESTIONS AND showing genuine interest in others are key components of effective conversation. They demonstrate that you value the other person's perspective and encourage deeper connections.

1. Types of Questions

DIFFERENT TYPES OF questions can serve various purposes in a conversation. Understanding when and how to use each type can enhance your conversational skills.

Open-Ended Questions

OPEN-ENDED QUESTIONS invite the other person to elaborate and provide more detailed responses. They are ideal for encouraging dialogue and exploring topics in depth. Examples include:

- "What inspired you to pursue your career?"

- "How do you spend your weekends?"

- "What are your thoughts on [current event/topic]?"

Closed-Ended Questions

CLOSED-ENDED QUESTIONS can be answered with a simple "yes" or "no" or a brief response. They are useful for gathering specific information or confirming details but should be balanced with open-ended questions to avoid stalling the conversation. Examples include:

- "Do you enjoy working here?"

- "Have you visited this place before?"

- "Is this your first time at this event?"

Follow-Up Questions

FOLLOW-UP QUESTIONS show that you are actively listening and interested in learning more. They build on the other person's previous response and encourage them to share further. Examples include:

- "That's fascinating. Can you tell me more about how you got involved in that project?"

- "I didn't know you traveled to [destination]. What was your experience like there?"

- "You mentioned you enjoy reading. What books have had the biggest impact on you?"

Reflective Questions

REFLECTIVE QUESTIONS encourage the other person to think more deeply about their experiences, feelings, or opinions. They often start with phrases like "How do you feel about..." or "What do you think about..." Examples include:

- "How do you feel about the changes in the industry?"

- "What do you think are the biggest challenges in your field?"

- "How has your perspective on this issue evolved over time?"

2. Showing Genuine Interest

GENUINE INTEREST IS the foundation of meaningful conversations. It involves being curious about the other person's experiences, opinions, and emotions and expressing that curiosity authentically.

Active Listening

AS MENTIONED EARLIER, active listening is crucial for showing genuine interest. By focusing on the speaker and responding empathetically, you demonstrate that you value their perspective.

Body Language

YOUR BODY LANGUAGE can convey interest and engagement. Maintain eye contact, nod in agreement, and use open and inviting gestures. Avoid crossing your arms or appearing distracted.

Encouraging Participation

ENCOURAGE THE OTHER person to share more by using phrases like "Tell me more about that," "I'm curious to hear your thoughts," or "What was that experience like for you?" These prompts signal that you are interested in their story.

Validating Emotions

ACKNOWLEDGE AND VALIDATE the other person's emotions by saying things like "That sounds really exciting," "I can see why that would be frustrating," or "It must have been rewarding to achieve that." Validating emotions fosters a deeper connection and makes the other person feel understood.

3. Deepening the Conversation

TO MAKE CONVERSATIONS more meaningful, aim to go beyond surface-level topics and explore deeper subjects that reveal more about the other person's values, beliefs, and experiences.

Personal Stories

SHARE PERSONAL STORIES that relate to the topic at hand. Personal stories create a sense of intimacy and encourage the other person to share their own experiences.

Shared Values

DISCUSS SHARED VALUES and beliefs to create a sense of connection. Conversations about values can be deeply meaningful and help you understand the other person on a more profound level.

Exploring Passions

ASK ABOUT THE OTHER person's passions and interests. People are often eager to talk about what they love, and these conversations can be highly engaging. Examples include:

- "What hobbies are you passionate about?"

- "What motivates you in your career?"

- "What causes or issues are you most passionate about?"

Discussing Challenges and Growth

CONVERSATIONS ABOUT challenges and personal growth can be deeply impactful. They provide insight into the other person's resilience, problem-solving abilities, and personal journey. Examples include:

- "What challenges have you faced in your career, and how did you overcome them?"

- "How have you grown from your experiences?"

- "What lessons have you learned from difficult situations?"

Tips for Making Meaningful Connections Through Dialogue

MAKING MEANINGFUL CONNECTIONS through dialogue requires intentionality, empathy, and a genuine desire to understand and connect with others. The following tips can help you foster deeper and more meaningful connections in your conversations.

1. Be Authentic

Authenticity is the key to building trust and rapport. Be genuine in your interactions, and let your true personality shine through. Avoid trying to impress or conform to what you think others want to hear. Authenticity fosters deeper connections and makes conversations more enjoyable for both parties.

2. Show Vulnerability

Showing vulnerability can create a sense of intimacy and trust. Share your own experiences, challenges, and emotions openly. Vulnerability encourages the other person to do the same, leading to more meaningful and honest conversations.

3. Practice Empathy

EMPATHY IS THE ABILITY to understand and share the feelings of others. Practice empathy by actively listening, validating emotions, and responding with compassion. Empathetic conversations create a safe space for sharing and foster deeper connections.

4. Be Present

BEING FULLY PRESENT in the conversation is essential for making meaningful connections. Avoid distractions and focus on the other person. Being present shows that you value the conversation and the other person, enhancing the quality of the interaction.

5. Ask Thoughtful Questions

THOUGHTFUL QUESTIONS demonstrate genuine interest and encourage the other person to share more deeply. Avoid superficial questions and instead ask about their experiences, values, and passions. Thoughtful questions lead to more meaningful and engaging conversations.

6. Listen More Than You Speak

AIM TO LISTEN MORE than you speak in conversations. Listening allows you to understand the other person's perspective and respond thoughtfully. It also shows that you value their input and are interested in what they have to say.

7. Use Positive Language

POSITIVE LANGUAGE CREATES a constructive and supportive atmosphere. Focus on what can be done rather than what cannot. Use encouraging and affirming words and phrases. Positive language fosters a sense of optimism and connection.

8. Find Common Interests

FINDING COMMON INTERESTS creates a sense of connection and shared experience. Look for topics or activities that you both enjoy and explore them together. Common interests provide a foundation for deeper conversations and lasting connections.

9. Respect Differences

RESPECTING DIFFERENCES is crucial for meaningful connections. Acknowledge and appreciate the other person's unique perspective and experiences. Avoid judgment or criticism and instead seek to understand and learn from their viewpoint.

10. Follow Up

FOLLOWING UP ON PREVIOUS conversations shows that you care and are invested in the relationship. Remembering details and checking in on the other person's progress or experiences demonstrates thoughtfulness and deepens the connection. For example:

- "Last time we spoke, you mentioned a project you were working on. How's it going?"

- "I remember you were planning a trip. How was it?"

- "You mentioned a book you were reading. What did you think of it?"

Personal Stories and Case Studies

TO ILLUSTRATE THE IMPACT of effective conversation techniques, let's explore some personal stories and case studies.

Case Study 1: Sarah's Journey to Meaningful Connections

SARAH, A 30-YEAR-OLD graphic designer, struggled with starting and sustaining conversations at social events. She often felt anxious and unsure of how to engage with others. Sarah decided to work with a communication coach to improve her conversation skills.

Through coaching, Sarah learned the importance of active listening, asking open-ended questions, and showing genuine interest. She practiced these techniques at networking events and social gatherings. Sarah also focused on being authentic and showing vulnerability in her interactions.

Over time, Sarah's confidence grew, and she began to form more meaningful connections. She found that people responded positively to her genuine interest and empathetic listening. Sarah's improved conversation skills enriched her personal and professional relationships.

Case Study 2: James's Transformation through Empathetic Dialogue

JAMES, A 35-YEAR-OLD sales executive, faced challenges in connecting with clients and colleagues. He often struggled to build rapport and felt that his conversations lacked depth. James decided to attend a communication workshop to enhance his conversational skills.

At the workshop, James learned the art of asking thoughtful questions and showing empathy. He practiced using open-ended questions, reflective questions, and empathetic responses. James also focused on being present and fully engaged in his conversations.

James's transformation was remarkable. He became more adept at initiating and sustaining meaningful conversations. His ability to connect with clients and colleagues on a deeper level led to increased sales, stronger professional relationships, and a more fulfilling social life.

Personal Story: Emily's Path to Authentic Connections

EMILY, A 27-YEAR-OLD teacher, struggled with making meaningful connections at social events. She often felt nervous and unsure of how to engage with others. Emily decided to seek guidance from a mentor to improve her conversation skills.

Through mentoring, Emily learned the importance of authenticity, empathy, and active listening. She practiced being genuine in her interactions, showing vulnerability, and asking thoughtful questions. Emily also focused on finding common interests and respecting differences.

Emily's path to authentic connections led to significant improvements. She became more confident in social interactions and formed deeper relationships with colleagues and friends. Emily's journey to effective conversation techniques enriched her personal and professional life.

Conclusion

Effective conversation techniques are essential for building strong relationships, fostering meaningful connections, and navigating social interactions with confidence. By learning how to start and sustain conversations, mastering the art of asking questions and showing interest, and following tips for making meaningful connections through dialogue, individuals can enhance their social competence and enrich their personal and professional lives.

Personal stories and case studies demonstrate that transformation is possible with the right strategies and mindset. As you continue reading this book, remember that developing effective conversation techniques is an ongoing journey that requires patience, practice, and self-compassion. By embracing this journey and applying the insights and techniques discussed, you can develop the conversational skills needed to thrive in both personal and professional settings. Let's move forward together, step by step, towards more meaningful, engaging, and effective conversations.

Chapter 8: Non-Verbal Communication Mastery

Understanding Body Language and Its Impact

Non-verbal communication, or body language, plays a crucial role in our interactions. It encompasses all the ways we convey messages without using words, such as facial expressions, gestures, posture, and eye contact. Understanding and mastering non-verbal communication can significantly enhance your ability to connect with others, interpret their intentions, and project confidence and competence.

The Importance of Non-Verbal Communication

NON-VERBAL COMMUNICATION often carries more weight than verbal communication. Research suggests that up to 93% of communication effectiveness is determined by non-verbal cues, with 55% attributed to body language and 38% to tone of voice. This highlights the importance of paying attention to non-verbal signals in our interactions.

Types of Non-Verbal Communication

NON-VERBAL COMMUNICATION can be categorized into several types, each playing a distinct role in how we convey and interpret messages:

1. Facial Expressions

Facial expressions are one of the most powerful forms of non-verbal communication. They can convey a wide range of emotions, from happiness and surprise to anger and sadness. Facial expressions are often universal, meaning that people from different cultures can usually recognize and interpret them similarly.

2. Gestures

Gestures are movements of the hands, arms, or other parts of the body that communicate specific messages. They can be used to emphasize points, indicate directions, or express emotions. While some gestures are universally understood, others can have different meanings in different cultures.

3. Posture

Posture refers to how we position our bodies when standing or sitting. It can convey confidence, openness, defensiveness, or submissiveness. Open and relaxed postures often indicate confidence and approachability, while closed or tense postures may suggest discomfort or defensiveness.

4. Eye Contact

Eye contact is a critical component of non-verbal communication. It can convey interest, attention, confidence, and respect. However, the appropriateness of eye contact can vary across cultures. In some cultures, direct eye contact is seen as a sign of confidence and honesty, while in others, it may be considered disrespectful or confrontational.

5. Proxemics

Proxemics refers to the use of personal space in communication. The distance we maintain from others can convey intimacy, formality, or aggression. Personal space preferences can vary based on cultural norms, individual preferences, and the nature of the relationship.

6. Touch

Touch is another powerful form of non-verbal communication. It can convey comfort, support, affection, or authority. The meaning of touch can depend on the context, relationship, and cultural norms.

7. Paralanguage

Paralanguage includes the non-verbal elements of speech, such as tone, pitch, volume, and speech rate. These elements can significantly impact how a message is received and interpreted. For example, a warm and enthusiastic tone can convey friendliness and interest, while a monotone voice may suggest boredom or indifference.

Impact of Non-Verbal Communication

NON-VERBAL COMMUNICATION impacts various aspects of our interactions, including:

1. Conveying Emotions

Non-verbal cues are often more effective than words at conveying emotions. Facial expressions, tone of voice, and gestures can reveal feelings that might not be expressed verbally. For example, a smile can indicate happiness, while crossed arms might suggest defensiveness.

2. Building Rapport and Trust

Effective non-verbal communication can help build rapport and trust. Positive body language, such as maintaining eye contact and open gestures, can create a sense of connection and mutual understanding. Conversely, negative body language, such as avoiding eye contact or fidgeting, can undermine trust and rapport.

3. Enhancing Verbal Messages

Non-verbal cues can enhance or contradict verbal messages. Consistent and aligned non-verbal communication reinforces the spoken word, making the message more credible and impactful. Inconsistent non-verbal cues, however, can create confusion and mistrust.

4. Regulating Conversations

Non-verbal communication plays a crucial role in regulating conversations. Cues such as nodding, maintaining eye contact, and using hand gestures can indicate when it is appropriate to speak or listen. They help manage the flow of conversation and ensure smooth communication.

Tips for Improving Your Own Body Language

IMPROVING YOUR OWN body language involves becoming aware of your non-verbal cues and practicing techniques that project confidence, openness, and approachability. The following tips can help you enhance your body language for more effective communication.

1. Maintain Good Posture

Good posture conveys confidence and openness. Practice standing and sitting up straight with your shoulders back and your weight evenly distributed. Avoid slouching or leaning excessively, as these postures can indicate a lack of confidence or interest.

2. Use Open Gestures

Open gestures, such as keeping your arms uncrossed and your hands visible, signal approachability and openness. Avoid crossing your arms or hiding your hands, as these gestures can be perceived as defensive or closed off.

3. Make Eye Contact

Eye contact is a powerful way to convey confidence and interest. Aim to maintain steady eye contact with the person you are speaking to, but avoid staring, which can be uncomfortable. Use eye contact to show that you are engaged and attentive.

4. Smile Genuinely

A genuine smile can convey warmth, friendliness, and approachability. Practice smiling naturally, with your eyes crinkling slightly. Avoid forced or insincere smiles, as they can be perceived as disingenuous.

5. Mirror and Match

Mirroring and matching the other person's body language can create a sense of rapport and connection. Subtly mimic their gestures, posture, and tone of voice to show that you are in sync with them. Be careful not to overdo it, as excessive mirroring can come across as insincere or manipulative.

6. Use Hand Gestures

Hand gestures can enhance your verbal messages and make your communication more dynamic. Use gestures to emphasize key points and illustrate concepts. Avoid excessive or distracting hand movements, and be mindful of cultural differences in the interpretation of gestures.

7. Be Aware of Personal Space

Respect personal space and be mindful of cultural differences in personal space preferences. Maintain an appropriate distance based on the context and relationship. Avoid standing too close or too far, as this can create discomfort or detachment.

8. Control Nervous Habits

Nervous habits, such as fidgeting, tapping your foot, or playing with objects, can detract from your message and make you appear anxious. Practice controlling these habits by becoming aware of them and finding ways to manage anxiety, such as deep breathing or grounding techniques.

9. Use Your Voice Effectively

Your tone of voice, pitch, volume, and speech rate all contribute to your non-verbal communication. Practice using a warm and enthusiastic tone, varying your pitch and volume to maintain interest, and speaking at a moderate pace to ensure clarity. Avoid a monotone voice, as it can be perceived as boring or disinterested.

10. Practice Self-Awareness

Regularly reflect on your body language and seek feedback from others. Practice self-awareness by observing your non-verbal cues in different situations and making adjustments as needed. Recording yourself during practice conversations can also help you identify areas for improvement.

Reading and Interpreting Others' Non-Verbal Cues

UNDERSTANDING AND INTERPRETING others' non-verbal cues is essential for effective communication and building meaningful connections. The following techniques can help you read and interpret non-verbal cues accurately.

1. Observe Baseline Behavior

To accurately interpret non-verbal cues, it is important to establish a baseline of the other person's typical behavior. Observe how they usually sit, stand, gesture, and express emotions. This baseline helps you identify deviations that may indicate specific feelings or reactions.

2. Look for Congruence

Pay attention to the congruence between verbal and non-verbal messages. When verbal and non-verbal cues align, the message is more likely to be genuine and credible. Incongruence, such as saying "I'm fine" while displaying a sad expression, may indicate that the person is not being entirely truthful or comfortable.

3. Focus on Clusters of Cues

Interpret non-verbal cues in clusters rather than in isolation. A single gesture or expression may not provide enough context to accurately understand the message. Look for patterns and combinations of cues that reinforce or contradict each other.

4. Consider Context

The context of the interaction is crucial for interpreting non-verbal cues accurately. Consider the setting, relationship, and cultural norms when analyzing body language. For example, a person's behavior in a formal business meeting may differ from their behavior in a casual social gathering.

5. Pay Attention to Facial Expressions

Facial expressions are rich sources of emotional information. Observe changes in the person's facial expressions, such as smiling, frowning, or furrowing their brows. These expressions can provide insights into their emotional state and reactions.

6. Watch for Microexpressions

Microexpressions are brief, involuntary facial expressions that reveal genuine emotions. They can occur in a fraction of a second and are often difficult to control. Watching for microexpressions can help you detect underlying emotions, even if the person is trying to conceal them.

7. Notice Changes in Posture

Changes in posture can indicate shifts in the person's comfort level or attitude. For example, leaning forward may signal interest and engagement, while leaning back or crossing arms may suggest defensiveness or disinterest. Pay attention to these changes and consider their context.

8. Interpret Eye Contact

Eye contact can convey a range of emotions and intentions. Consistent eye contact generally indicates confidence, interest, and attentiveness. Avoiding eye contact may suggest discomfort, anxiety, or deception. However, cultural differences in eye contact norms should also be considered.

9. Analyze Gestures

Gestures can provide valuable information about the person's thoughts and feelings. Observe their hand movements, pointing, and other gestures. For example, open palm gestures often indicate honesty and openness, while clenched fists may suggest anger or tension.

10. Consider Paralanguage

Paralanguage elements, such as tone, pitch, volume, and speech rate, can enhance your understanding of the person's message. A warm and enthusiastic tone may indicate excitement, while a flat and monotone voice may suggest boredom or detachment. Changes in these elements can also signal shifts in emotion.

11. Recognize Signs of Nervousness

Signs of nervousness, such as fidgeting, tapping, or avoiding eye contact, can indicate anxiety or discomfort. Recognizing these signs can help you adjust your approach to make the person feel more at ease.

12. Use Empathy and Intuition

Empathy and intuition play important roles in interpreting non-verbal cues. Put yourself in the other person's shoes and consider how they might be feeling based on their body language. Trust your instincts and be sensitive to subtle signals that may reveal their emotional state.

Personal Stories and Case Studies

TO ILLUSTRATE THE IMPACT of mastering non-verbal communication, let's explore some personal stories and case studies.

Case Study 1: Tom's Journey to Confident Body Language

TOM, A 34-YEAR-OLD project manager, struggled with projecting confidence in meetings and presentations. He often found himself slouching, avoiding eye contact, and fidgeting, which undermined his message and credibility. Tom decided to work with a body language coach to improve his non-verbal communication.

Through coaching, Tom learned to maintain good posture, make steady eye contact, and use open gestures. He practiced these techniques in front of a mirror and recorded his practice presentations to identify areas for improvement. Tom also focused on controlling nervous habits by using deep breathing and grounding techniques.

Over time, Tom's body language improved significantly. He projected confidence and authority in his meetings and presentations, which led to greater respect and trust from his colleagues. Tom's enhanced non-verbal communication skills contributed to his professional success and personal growth.

Case Study 2: Sarah's Transformation through Non-Verbal Cues

SARAH, A 28-YEAR-OLD sales executive, faced challenges in interpreting her clients' non-verbal cues. She often missed subtle signals that could have provided valuable insights into their needs and preferences. Sarah decided to attend a workshop on non-verbal communication to enhance her skills.

At the workshop, Sarah learned to observe baseline behavior, focus on clusters of cues, and consider context. She practiced interpreting facial expressions, microexpressions, and changes in posture. Sarah also developed her empathy and intuition to better understand her clients' emotions.

Sarah's transformation was remarkable. She became more adept at reading her clients' non-verbal cues, which improved her ability to tailor her sales approach and build rapport. Her enhanced non-verbal communication skills led to increased sales, stronger client relationships, and a more fulfilling career.

Personal Story: Emily's Path to Non-Verbal Communication Mastery

EMILY, A 30-YEAR-OLD teacher, struggled with connecting with her students and colleagues due to her limited non-verbal communication skills. She often felt that her messages were misunderstood or ignored. Emily decided to seek guidance from a mentor to improve her non-verbal communication.

Through mentoring, Emily learned the importance of body language, facial expressions, and tone of voice. She practiced maintaining good posture, using open gestures, and making eye contact. Emily also focused on interpreting her students' and colleagues' non-verbal cues to better understand their needs and emotions.

Emily's path to non-verbal communication mastery led to significant improvements. She became more effective in her teaching and built stronger relationships with her students and colleagues. Emily's journey to mastering non-verbal communication enriched her professional and personal life.

Conclusion

Mastering non-verbal communication is essential for effective interactions, building strong relationships, and navigating social situations with confidence. By understanding the impact of body language, improving your own non-verbal cues, and reading and interpreting others' non-verbal signals, you can enhance your communication skills and make meaningful connections.

Personal stories and case studies demonstrate that transformation is possible with the right strategies and mindset. As you continue reading this book, remember that mastering non-verbal communication is an ongoing journey that requires patience, practice, and self-compassion. By embracing this journey and applying the insights and techniques discussed, you can develop the non-verbal communication skills needed to thrive in both personal and professional settings. Let's move forward together, step by step, towards more confident, engaging, and effective non-verbal communication.

Chapter 9: Social Etiquette and Manners

Importance of Social Etiquette in Different Contexts

Social etiquette encompasses the conventional norms and behaviors that govern interactions in society. It plays a crucial role in ensuring smooth, respectful, and pleasant interactions in various social contexts. Understanding and practicing good etiquette helps individuals navigate social landscapes with confidence and grace, fostering positive relationships and minimizing conflicts.

1. Building and Maintaining Relationships

Good social etiquette is fundamental in building and maintaining relationships, whether personal or professional. It reflects a person's respect and consideration for others, which is essential for trust and rapport. Polite and respectful behavior helps create a positive atmosphere, making interactions more enjoyable and meaningful.

2. Professional Success

In professional settings, social etiquette is indispensable. It influences how colleagues, clients, and superiors perceive an individual, impacting career growth and opportunities. Professional etiquette encompasses everything from dressing appropriately and punctuality to effective communication and networking skills. Adhering to these norms can enhance one's reputation and credibility, paving the way for career advancement.

3. Cultural Sensitivity and Global Interactions

In our increasingly globalized world, understanding and respecting cultural differences in etiquette is vital. Different cultures have distinct social norms, and being aware of these can prevent misunderstandings and foster cross-cultural relationships. Cultural sensitivity in etiquette demonstrates respect for diverse traditions and practices, promoting harmonious interactions in international contexts.

4. Social Harmony and Conflict Resolution

Practicing good etiquette can help maintain social harmony and facilitate conflict resolution. Respectful communication and behavior reduce the likelihood of misunderstandings and confrontations. When conflicts do arise, a foundation of good etiquette allows for more constructive and respectful dialogue, making it easier to reach amicable solutions.

5. Personal Confidence and Comfort

Knowing and practicing social etiquette can boost personal confidence and comfort in various social situations. Understanding what is expected in different contexts reduces anxiety and uncertainty, allowing individuals to engage more freely and confidently. This confidence can enhance the quality of interactions and contribute to a positive social experience.

Guidelines for Polite and Respectful Interactions

POLITE AND RESPECTFUL interactions are the cornerstone of good social etiquette. The following guidelines provide practical advice for navigating social situations with courtesy and respect.

1. Greeting and Introductions

Proper Greetings

- USE APPROPRIATE GREETINGS for the context, such as "Good morning," "Hello," or "Hi."

- Smile and make eye contact to convey friendliness and openness.

- In formal settings, use titles and last names unless invited to use first names.

Introducing Yourself

- CLEARLY STATE YOUR name and offer a handshake (if culturally appropriate).

- Provide a brief, relevant detail about yourself to initiate conversation, such as your job title or role in a social event.

Introducing Others

- INTRODUCE PEOPLE BY stating their names and providing relevant context about how you know them or their relationship to the group.

- Include a brief, positive detail about each person to facilitate further conversation.

2. Active Listening and Engagement

Show Interest

- MAKE EYE CONTACT AND nod occasionally to show you are listening.

- Avoid interrupting and allow the speaker to finish their thoughts.

- Use verbal affirmations like "I see," "That's interesting," or "Tell me more."

Ask Questions

- ASK OPEN-ENDED QUESTIONS to encourage the speaker to elaborate.

- Follow up on previous comments to show genuine interest and engagement.

Avoid Distractions

- PUT AWAY ELECTRONIC devices and give the speaker your full attention.

- Avoid looking around the room or appearing disinterested.

3. Respectful Communication

Use Polite Language

- USE "PLEASE," "THANK you," "excuse me," and "I'm sorry" as appropriate.

- Address people respectfully, using titles and last names in formal settings.

Be Mindful of Tone

- MAINTAIN A FRIENDLY and respectful tone, even in disagreements.

- Avoid raising your voice or using aggressive language.

Non-Verbal Communication

- USE POSITIVE BODY language, such as smiling and nodding.

- Maintain an open posture and avoid crossing your arms or turning away from the speaker.

4. Table Manners

Basic Table Etiquette

- WAIT FOR THE HOST to indicate when it is time to start eating.

- Use utensils properly and avoid speaking with your mouth full.

- Place your napkin on your lap and use it to dab your mouth as needed.

Serving and Passing Food

- OFFER TO SERVE OTHERS before serving yourself.

- Pass dishes to the right and avoid reaching across the table.

Handling Utensils and Glassware

- HOLD UTENSILS CORRECTLY and use them appropriately for each course.

- Hold your glass by the stem to avoid warming the contents with your hand.

5. Punctuality and Time Management

Arriving on Time

- ARRIVE ON TIME FOR appointments, meetings, and social events.

- If you are running late, inform the host or relevant parties as soon as possible.

Respecting Others' Time

- KEEP CONVERSATIONS and meetings concise and to the point.

- Avoid monopolizing conversations or speaking for too long.

6. Giving and Receiving Compliments

Offering Compliments

- BE SINCERE AND SPECIFIC when giving compliments.

- Focus on positive qualities or achievements rather than superficial traits.

Receiving Compliments

- ACCEPT COMPLIMENTS graciously with a simple "thank you."

- Avoid deflecting or downplaying the compliment.

7. Handling Conflicts and Disagreements

Stay Calm and Composed

- REMAIN CALM AND COMPOSED during conflicts and disagreements.

- Take deep breaths and avoid raising your voice.

Listen and Acknowledge

- LISTEN TO THE OTHER person's perspective and acknowledge their feelings.

- Avoid interrupting and show empathy.

Seek Common Ground

- FOCUS ON FINDING COMMON ground and mutually acceptable solutions.

- Avoid personal attacks and stay focused on the issue at hand.

Adapting Etiquette to Various Social Situations

DIFFERENT SOCIAL CONTEXTS require different approaches to etiquette. Adapting your behavior to the specific situation demonstrates awareness and respect for social norms. The following sections provide guidelines for adapting etiquette in various settings.

1. Professional Settings

Meetings and Conferences

- ARRIVE ON TIME AND be prepared with any necessary materials.

- Introduce yourself and others politely and professionally.

- Participate actively but avoid dominating the conversation.

- Respect the meeting agenda and stay on topic.

Networking Events

- APPROACH PEOPLE WITH a friendly and open demeanor.

- Use appropriate ice breakers to initiate conversations.

- Exchange business cards respectfully and follow up on connections.

- Avoid monopolizing conversations and give others a chance to speak.

Email and Written Communication

- USE PROFESSIONAL LANGUAGE and proper grammar.

- Start with a polite greeting and end with a courteous closing.

- Be concise and clear in your messages.

- Respond to emails in a timely manner.

2. Social Gatherings

Dinner Parties

- RSVP PROMPTLY AND inform the host of any dietary restrictions.

- Bring a small gift, such as wine or flowers, to thank the host.

- Engage in polite conversation and avoid controversial topics.

- Offer to help with setting up or cleaning up after the meal.

Casual Get-Togethers

- BE RESPECTFUL OF THE host's home and property.

- Engage with other guests and make an effort to include everyone in the conversation.

- Follow the host's lead regarding activities and schedule.

- Express gratitude to the host before leaving.

Cultural and Religious Events

- FAMILIARIZE YOURSELF with the customs and traditions of the event.

- Dress appropriately and follow any specific dress codes.

- Participate respectfully and observe any rituals or practices.

- Ask questions if you are unsure about proper behavior.

3. Digital Communication

Social Media

- BE MINDFUL OF THE content you share and its potential impact on others.

- Respect others' privacy and avoid sharing sensitive information without permission.

- Engage positively and avoid online arguments or negative comments.

- Be considerate of different perspectives and avoid offensive language.

Text Messaging

- Use proper grammar and punctuation to ensure clarity.

- Avoid sending multiple messages in quick succession.

- Respect others' time and avoid texting late at night or during inappropriate times.

- Use emojis and abbreviations appropriately based on the relationship and context.

Video Calls and Virtual Meetings

- ENSURE YOUR BACKGROUND is clean and professional.

- Dress appropriately and be mindful of your appearance.

- Mute your microphone when not speaking to avoid background noise.

- Use the video feature to maintain visual engagement, if appropriate.

4. Travel and Public Spaces

Airports and Airplanes

- FOLLOW SECURITY PROCEDURES and be respectful to staff.

- Be considerate of other passengers by keeping noise to a minimum.

- Respect personal space and avoid reclining your seat too far back.

- Follow the airline's rules and guidelines.

Public Transportation

- OFFER YOUR SEAT TO elderly, disabled, or pregnant passengers.

- Keep your belongings out of the aisle and off other seats.

- Avoid loud conversations or phone calls.

- Respect others' personal space and hygiene.

Hotels and Accommodations

- BE POLITE AND RESPECTFUL to hotel staff.

- Follow the hotel's rules and guidelines, including check-in and check-out times.

- Keep noise levels down, especially during late hours.

- Tip housekeeping staff appropriately for their services.

5. Family Gatherings

Respecting Family Traditions

- PARTICIPATE IN FAMILY traditions and rituals with respect and enthusiasm.

- Be considerate of different family members' preferences and needs.

- Offer to help with preparations and clean-up.

Handling Conflicts

- ADDRESS CONFLICTS calmly and respectfully, focusing on resolution.

- Avoid bringing up contentious topics that could lead to arguments.

- Show empathy and understanding for different viewpoints.

Expressing Gratitude

- SHOW APPRECIATION for the effort family members put into organizing gatherings.

- Thank family members for their hospitality and company.

- Follow up with a thank-you note or message after the event.

Personal Stories and Case Studies

TO ILLUSTRATE THE IMPORTANCE and application of social etiquette, let's explore some personal stories and case studies.

Case Study 1: David's Journey to Professional Etiquette

DAVID, A 35-YEAR-OLD marketing manager, struggled with professional etiquette in meetings and networking events. He often felt uncertain about how to introduce himself and engage with colleagues. David decided to attend a professional development workshop to improve his etiquette skills.

Through the workshop, David learned the importance of proper greetings, active listening, and respectful communication. He practiced introducing himself confidently, using open-ended questions to engage others, and maintaining a professional demeanor. David also focused on punctuality and effective email communication.

David's journey to professional etiquette led to significant improvements. He became more confident in meetings and networking events, building stronger relationships with colleagues and clients. David's enhanced professional etiquette contributed to his career success and personal growth.

Case Study 2: Sarah's Transformation through Social Etiquette

SARAH, A 28-YEAR-OLD teacher, faced challenges in social gatherings due to her limited understanding of social etiquette. She often felt anxious and unsure of how to interact with others at events. Sarah decided to work with a social coach to improve her etiquette skills.

Through coaching, Sarah learned the importance of proper greetings, polite conversation, and respectful behavior. She practiced active listening, giving and receiving compliments, and handling conflicts gracefully. Sarah also focused on adapting her behavior to different social contexts, such as dinner parties and cultural events.

Sarah's transformation was remarkable. She became more confident and comfortable in social gatherings, forming meaningful connections with others. Her improved social etiquette enriched her personal and professional relationships.

Personal Story: Emily's Path to Cultural Sensitivity

EMILY, A 30-YEAR-OLD business executive, struggled with cultural sensitivity in her international interactions. She often felt uncertain about proper behavior and etiquette in different cultural contexts. Emily decided to seek guidance from a cultural etiquette expert to enhance her skills.

Through guidance, Emily learned the importance of understanding and respecting cultural differences in etiquette. She studied the customs and traditions of the cultures she interacted with, practiced appropriate greetings, and adapted her communication style. Emily also focused on showing empathy and avoiding cultural faux pas.

Emily's path to cultural sensitivity led to significant improvements. She became more adept at navigating cross-cultural interactions, building stronger relationships with international clients and colleagues. Emily's journey to cultural sensitivity enriched her professional and personal life.

Conclusion

Social etiquette and manners are essential for effective interactions, building strong relationships, and navigating various social contexts with confidence and grace. By understanding the importance of social etiquette, following guidelines for polite and respectful interactions, and adapting behavior to different situations, individuals can enhance their social competence and enrich their personal and professional lives.

Personal stories and case studies demonstrate that transformation is possible with the right strategies and mindset. As you continue reading this book, remember that mastering social etiquette is an ongoing journey that requires patience, practice, and self-compassion. By embracing this journey and applying the insights and techniques discussed, you can develop the etiquette skills needed to thrive in both personal and professional settings. Let's move forward together, step by step, towards more respectful, engaging, and effective social interactions.

Chapter 10: Networking and Building Relationships

Strategies for Effective Networking

Networking is an essential skill for personal and professional growth. It involves establishing and nurturing relationships that can provide support, opportunities, and collaboration. Effective networking is not just about making contacts but about building meaningful connections that can benefit all parties involved.

1. Understanding the Purpose of Networking

Before diving into strategies, it's important to understand why networking is crucial. Networking can help you:

- Gain new perspectives and ideas.

- Discover opportunities for career advancement.

- Find mentors and advisors.

- Build a support system for personal and professional challenges.

- Increase visibility within your industry or community.

2. Setting Clear Networking Goals

Effective networking begins with clear goals. Knowing what you want to achieve helps you focus your efforts and measure your progress. Consider the following questions:

- What are your short-term and long-term career goals?

- What kind of support or connections do you need to achieve these goals?

- What specific skills or knowledge are you seeking?

3. Identifying Networking Opportunities

Networking opportunities are everywhere. Recognizing and utilizing these opportunities is key to effective networking. Some common places to network include:

- Professional associations and industry conferences.

- Social events and community gatherings.

- Online platforms like LinkedIn and industry-specific forums.

- Educational settings, such as workshops and seminars.

- Workplace events and informal gatherings.

4. Preparing for Networking Events

Preparation is crucial for successful networking. Here are some tips to help you get ready:

- Research: Learn about the event, the attendees, and the speakers. This will help you identify potential connections and conversation topics.

- Prepare Your Elevator Pitch: An elevator pitch is a concise summary of who you are, what you do, and what you are looking for. It should be engaging and memorable.

- Bring Business Cards: Business cards are a professional way to share your contact information. Make sure they are up-to-date and of good quality.

- Dress Appropriately: Dress in a way that aligns with the event's formality and makes you feel confident.

5. Starting Conversations

Starting conversations can be daunting, but with practice, it becomes easier. Here are some strategies:

- Use Ice Breakers: Simple ice breakers, such as commenting on the event or venue, can help start a conversation.

- Ask Open-Ended Questions: Questions that require more than a yes or no answer encourage dialogue. For example, "What brings you to this event?" or "How did you get started in your industry?"

- Show Genuine Interest: Listen actively and show curiosity about the other person's experiences and perspectives.

6. Building Rapport

Building rapport is about creating a connection and finding common ground. Here's how to build rapport effectively:

- Mirror Body Language: Subtly mirroring the other person's body language can create a sense of familiarity and comfort.

- Find Common Interests: Look for shared interests or experiences that can serve as a basis for further conversation.

- Be Authentic: Authenticity is key to building trust. Be yourself and show genuine interest in the other person.

7. Following Up

Following up is a critical step in networking. It reinforces the connection and opens the door for future interactions. Here's how to follow up effectively:

- Send a Thank-You Note: A brief thank-you email or message expressing your appreciation for the conversation can leave a positive impression.

- Reference Your Conversation: Mention something specific from your conversation to show that you were paying attention and valued the interaction.

- Suggest Future Interaction: Propose a coffee meeting, lunch, or another opportunity to continue the conversation.

Building and Maintaining Professional Relationships

BUILDING AND MAINTAINING professional relationships require ongoing effort and attention. Here are strategies to help you nurture these relationships over time.

1. Consistent Communication

Regular communication is essential for maintaining relationships. Here are some tips:

- Schedule Regular Check-Ins: Set reminders to check in with your contacts periodically. This could be through emails, phone calls, or face-to-face meetings.

- Share Relevant Information: Sending articles, news, or resources that might interest your contacts shows that you are thinking of them and value their interests.

- Celebrate Milestones: Acknowledge and celebrate your contacts' achievements, such as promotions, awards, or personal milestones.

2. Providing Value

Relationships are reciprocal. Providing value to your contacts fosters goodwill and strengthens the connection. Here's how to add value:

- Offer Help and Support: Be willing to assist your contacts with their projects, challenges, or goals. This could be through advice, introductions, or resources.

- Share Opportunities: Inform your contacts about job openings, partnerships, or other opportunities that might benefit them.

- Provide Feedback: Offering constructive feedback or insights can be valuable, especially when your contacts are seeking input.

3. Building Trust

Trust is the foundation of strong professional relationships. Here are ways to build and maintain trust:

- Be Reliable: Follow through on your commitments and be consistent in your actions.

- Maintain Confidentiality: Respect the confidentiality of your conversations and any sensitive information shared with you.

- Be Honest: Practice honesty and transparency in your interactions. Admit when you don't have the answers and avoid exaggerations.

4. Networking Within Your Organization

Networking isn't limited to external contacts; it's equally important to build relationships within your organization. Here's how:

- Engage with Colleagues: Take the time to get to know your colleagues beyond work tasks. Engage in conversations during breaks or social events.

- Collaborate on Projects: Volunteering for cross-departmental projects can help you build connections and demonstrate your skills.

- Seek Mentorship: Identify potential mentors within your organization and seek their guidance and support.

5. Joining Professional Associations

Professional associations offer a wealth of networking opportunities and resources. Here's how to make the most of them:

- Attend Events: Participate in association events, such as conferences, workshops, and social gatherings.

- Volunteer for Committees: Volunteering for committees or special projects can help you build connections and gain visibility.

- Utilize Online Platforms: Engage with your association's online platforms, such as forums, webinars, and social media groups.

6. Leveraging Social Media

Social media platforms, particularly LinkedIn, are powerful tools for building and maintaining professional relationships. Here's how to use them effectively:

- Create a Strong Profile: Ensure your profile is complete, professional, and reflects your brand. Include a professional photo, a compelling summary, and detailed work experience.

- Engage with Content: Share and comment on industry-related content to demonstrate your expertise and engage with your network.

- Connect Thoughtfully: When sending connection requests, personalize your message and explain why you'd like to connect.

7. Balancing Professional and Personal Relationships

While professional relationships are important, it's also valuable to build personal connections with your contacts. Here's how to balance both:

- Show Genuine Interest: Take an interest in your contacts' personal lives, such as their hobbies, family, or interests.

- Share Personal Stories: Share appropriate personal stories or experiences to create a more authentic connection.

- Respect Boundaries: Be mindful of personal boundaries and avoid prying into sensitive areas.

The Role of Trust and Reciprocity in Strong Connections

TRUST AND RECIPROCITY are fundamental principles in building and maintaining strong connections. They create a foundation for mutual respect, collaboration, and long-lasting relationships.

1. Understanding Trust in Relationships

Trust is the confidence that others will act with integrity, reliability, and fairness. It is built over time through consistent and positive interactions. Trust in professional relationships leads to:

- Increased Collaboration: Trust encourages open communication and teamwork.

- Greater Flexibility: Trust allows for more flexibility and autonomy in working relationships.

- Enhanced Problem-Solving: Trust fosters a safe environment for sharing ideas and addressing challenges.

2. Building Trust

Building trust involves consistent actions and behaviors that demonstrate your integrity and reliability. Here are strategies to build trust:

- Be Transparent: Practice transparency in your communication and actions. Share information openly and honestly.

- Deliver on Promises: Follow through on your commitments and deliver on your promises. Reliability builds trust.

- Admit Mistakes: Acknowledge and take responsibility for your mistakes. Apologize sincerely and take steps to rectify the situation.

- Show Respect: Treat others with respect and consideration. Respect for others' opinions, time, and boundaries builds trust.

3. The Principle of Reciprocity

Reciprocity is the mutual exchange of favors, support, and resources. It is a key principle in building strong relationships. When you help others, they are more likely to help you in return. Here's how to practice reciprocity:

- Offer Help Freely: Be generous with your time, knowledge, and resources. Help others without expecting immediate returns.

- Acknowledge Contributions: Recognize and appreciate the help and support you receive from others.

- Balance Give and Take: Ensure a balance between giving and receiving in your relationships. Avoid being overly dependent or excessively giving without reciprocation.

4. Fostering Mutual Respect

Mutual respect is a cornerstone of strong relationships. It involves recognizing and valuing each other's contributions, perspectives, and boundaries. Here's how to foster mutual respect:

- Listen Actively: Show genuine interest in others' opinions and experiences. Listen actively and acknowledge their contributions.

- Value Differences: Appreciate and respect differences in perspectives, skills, and backgrounds. Diversity enriches relationships.

- Communicate Respectfully: Use respectful language and tone in your communication. Avoid criticism, judgment, or condescension.

5. Developing Empathy

Empathy is the ability to understand and share the feelings of others. It plays a crucial role in building trust and strong connections. Here's how to develop empathy:

- Practice Active Listening: Listen with the intent to understand, not just to respond. Pay attention to verbal and non-verbal cues.

- Put Yourself in Their Shoes: Try to see situations from others' perspectives. Consider their feelings, experiences, and challenges.

- Express Understanding: Acknowledge others' feelings and show that you understand their perspective. Use empathetic statements like "I can see how that would be challenging."

6. Nurturing Long-Term Relationships

Building strong connections is an ongoing process that requires consistent effort and attention. Here's how to nurture long-term relationships:

- Stay in Touch: Maintain regular communication with your contacts. Check in periodically to show that you value the relationship.

- Celebrate Milestones: Acknowledge and celebrate important milestones and achievements in your contacts' lives.

- Offer Continuous Support: Be there for your contacts during both good times and challenging times. Offer support and encouragement when needed.

Personal Stories and Case Studies

TO ILLUSTRATE THE IMPACT of effective networking and building strong relationships, let's explore some personal stories and case studies.

Case Study 1: Jessica's Journey to Effective Networking

JESSICA, A 32-YEAR-old software developer, struggled with networking due to her introverted nature. She often felt uncomfortable initiating conversations and making connections at industry events. Jessica decided to work with a career coach to improve her networking skills.

Through coaching, Jessica learned to set clear networking goals, prepare her elevator pitch, and use open-ended questions to start conversations. She practiced active listening, showing genuine interest, and following up with contacts after events.

Jessica's journey to effective networking led to significant improvements. She became more confident in approaching people and initiating conversations. Her ability to build rapport and follow up with contacts resulted in valuable connections that helped her advance her career. Jessica's improved networking skills also enhanced her professional reputation and visibility within her industry.

Case Study 2: Michael's Transformation through Building

Professional Relationships

MICHAEL, A 40-YEAR-old financial analyst, faced challenges in building and maintaining professional relationships. He often struggled to keep in touch with contacts and provide value to his network. Michael decided to attend a professional development workshop focused on relationship-building skills.

At the workshop, Michael learned the importance of consistent communication, providing value, and building trust. He practiced scheduling regular check-ins, sharing relevant information, and offering help and support to his contacts. Michael also focused on leveraging social media platforms like LinkedIn to stay connected and engaged with his network.

Michael's transformation was remarkable. He became more proactive in maintaining his professional relationships, leading to stronger connections and increased opportunities. His ability to provide value and build trust enhanced his reputation and career prospects. Michael's journey to building professional relationships enriched his professional and personal life.

Personal Story: Emily's Path to Trust and Reciprocity

EMILY, A 28-YEAR-OLD marketing manager, struggled with building trust and reciprocity in her professional relationships. She often felt uncertain about how to establish trust and provide value to her contacts. Emily decided to seek guidance from a mentor to improve her relationship-building skills.

Through mentoring, Emily learned the importance of transparency, delivering on promises, and admitting mistakes. She practiced offering help freely, acknowledging contributions, and balancing give and take in her relationships. Emily also focused on developing empathy and fostering mutual respect.

Emily's path to trust and reciprocity led to significant improvements. She became more skilled at building and maintaining strong connections based on trust and mutual support. Her ability to offer help and value to her contacts resulted in reciprocal support and opportunities. Emily's journey to trust and reciprocity enriched her professional and personal relationships.

CONCLUSION

Networking and building strong relationships are essential for personal and professional success. By understanding the importance of networking, setting clear goals, and utilizing effective strategies, individuals can build meaningful connections that provide support, opportunities, and collaboration.

Building and maintaining professional relationships require consistent communication, providing value, and fostering trust and reciprocity. These principles create a foundation for mutual respect, collaboration, and long-lasting relationships.

Personal stories and case studies demonstrate that transformation is possible with the right strategies and mindset. As you continue reading this book, remember that networking and building relationships are ongoing journeys that require patience, practice, and self-compassion. By embracing this journey and applying the insights and techniques discussed, you can develop the networking and relationship-building skills needed to thrive in both personal and professional settings. Let's move forward together, step by step, towards more effective, engaging, and meaningful connections.

Chapter 11: Public Speaking and Presentation Skills

Overcoming Fear of Public Speaking

Public speaking is a common source of anxiety for many people. However, mastering this skill can open up numerous opportunities in both personal and professional life. Overcoming the fear of public speaking involves understanding the roots of this fear, developing confidence through preparation and practice, and using specific techniques to manage anxiety.

Understanding the Fear of Public Speaking

THE FEAR OF PUBLIC speaking, often referred to as glossophobia, can stem from various sources, including:

- Fear of Judgment: Worrying about how the audience will perceive you.

- Fear of Failure: Concern that you will make mistakes or forget your material.

- Lack of Experience: Feeling unprepared due to limited speaking experience.

- Negative Past Experiences: Previous experiences of public speaking that went poorly.

1. Changing Your Mindset

A SIGNIFICANT PART of overcoming the fear of public speaking involves changing your mindset. Here are some strategies:

- Reframe Your Thoughts: Instead of viewing public speaking as a performance, see it as a conversation or sharing of ideas. This can reduce pressure and make the experience feel more natural.

- Visualize Success: Spend time visualizing yourself delivering a successful presentation. Imagine the positive reactions from your audience and the sense of accomplishment you will feel.

- Embrace Nervousness: Accept that feeling nervous is normal and can be harnessed as energy to enhance your performance.

2. Building Confidence Through Preparation

PREPARATION IS KEY to building confidence and reducing anxiety. Here's how to prepare effectively:

- Know Your Material: Ensure you thoroughly understand your topic. This will make it easier to speak confidently and handle questions.

- Practice, Practice, Practice: Rehearse your presentation multiple times. Practice in front of a mirror, record yourself, or present to a trusted friend or family member for feedback.

- Organize Your Content: Structure your presentation with a clear beginning, middle, and end. Use an outline or note cards to keep your thoughts organized.

- Familiarize Yourself with the Venue: If possible, visit the venue beforehand to get comfortable with the space. This can reduce anxiety on the day of your presentation.

3. Managing Anxiety

TECHNIQUES FOR MANAGING anxiety can help you stay calm and focused. Here are some methods:

- Deep Breathing: Practice deep breathing exercises to calm your nerves. Breathe in slowly through your nose, hold for a few seconds, and exhale slowly through your mouth.

- Progressive Muscle Relaxation: Tense and relax different muscle groups in your body to release tension and promote relaxation.

- Positive Affirmations: Use positive affirmations to boost your confidence, such as "I am well-prepared and capable of delivering a great presentation."

- Mindfulness Meditation: Practice mindfulness meditation to stay present and focused. This can help reduce anxiety and improve concentration.

Techniques for Preparing and Delivering Effective Presentations

EFFECTIVE PRESENTATIONS require thorough preparation, clear organization, and engaging delivery. The following techniques can help you prepare and deliver presentations that captivate and inform your audience.

1. Preparing Your Presentation

Define Your Purpose

BEFORE YOU START CREATING your presentation, define its purpose. Ask yourself:

- What do I want to achieve with this presentation?

- What key message do I want to convey?

- Who is my audience, and what are their needs and expectations?

Research and Gather Information

CONDUCT THOROUGH RESEARCH to gather accurate and relevant information. Use credible sources and take detailed notes. Organize your information into categories to make it easier to structure your presentation.

Create an Outline

AN OUTLINE HELPS YOU organize your content logically. A typical outline includes:

- Introduction: Capture the audience's attention, introduce yourself, and state the purpose of your presentation.

- Main Points: Present your key points in a logical sequence. Use supporting evidence, such as statistics, quotes, and examples, to reinforce your message.

- Conclusion: Summarize your main points, restate the key message, and provide a call to action or closing remarks.

Design Visual Aids

VISUAL AIDS, SUCH AS slides, charts, and videos, can enhance your presentation and help convey information more effectively. Here are some tips for designing visual aids:

- Keep It Simple: Use clear and concise text, and avoid overcrowding your slides with too much information.

- Use High-Quality Images: Use high-quality images and graphics that are relevant to your content.

- Consistent Design: Maintain a consistent design throughout your presentation, including fonts, colors, and layout.

- Limit Text: Use bullet points or short sentences instead of long paragraphs. Aim for no more than 5-7 bullet points per slide.

Practice Delivery

PRACTICING YOUR DELIVERY is crucial for a smooth presentation. Here are some tips:

- Rehearse Out Loud: Practice speaking out loud to get comfortable with your material and improve your delivery.

- Time Yourself: Ensure your presentation fits within the allotted time. Adjust your content if necessary.

- Record Yourself: Recording yourself can help you identify areas for improvement, such as pacing, tone, and body language.

- Get Feedback: Present to a trusted friend or colleague and ask for constructive feedback.

2. Delivering Your Presentation

Engage Your Audience

ENGAGING YOUR AUDIENCE from the beginning is key to a successful presentation. Here's how:

- Start with a Hook: Use an interesting fact, a question, a quote, or a story to grab the audience's attention.

- Make Eye Contact: Maintain eye contact with different members of the audience to create a connection and show confidence.

- Use Gestures: Use natural gestures to emphasize points and convey enthusiasm.

- Move Around: Moving around the stage or room can help maintain the audience's interest. Avoid pacing or moving excessively, which can be distracting.

Communicate Clearly

CLEAR COMMUNICATION is essential for delivering an effective presentation. Here are some tips:

- Speak Clearly and Loudly: Ensure your voice is clear and loud enough to be heard by everyone in the audience. Avoid mumbling or speaking too quickly.

- Use Pauses: Use pauses to emphasize key points and give the audience time to absorb the information.

- Vary Your Tone: Vary your tone and pitch to maintain interest and convey emotion.

- Avoid Filler Words: Minimize the use of filler words, such as "um," "uh," and "like." Practice speaking smoothly and confidently.

Use Visual Aids Effectively

VISUAL AIDS CAN ENHANCE your presentation, but they should not overshadow your message. Here's how to use them effectively:

- Refer to Visuals: Refer to your visual aids when relevant, and explain how they support your points.

- Avoid Reading Slides: Do not read directly from your slides. Use them as prompts and speak naturally.

- Ensure Visibility: Ensure your visual aids are visible to everyone in the audience. Avoid standing in front of the screen or blocking the view.

Handle Questions Confidently

HANDLING QUESTIONS confidently demonstrates your expertise and engagement with the audience. Here's how to manage questions effectively:

- Invite Questions: Invite questions at the appropriate time, such as after each section or at the end of your presentation.

- Listen Carefully: Listen carefully to each question and make sure you understand it before responding.

- Stay Calm and Composed: Stay calm and composed, even if you don't know the answer. It's okay to say, "I don't know, but I can find out and get back to you."

- Acknowledge All Questions: Acknowledge all questions respectfully, even if they seem irrelevant or challenging.

3. Engaging and Connecting with Your Audience

ENGAGING AND CONNECTING with your audience is crucial for delivering an impactful presentation. The following techniques can help you build a strong connection and keep your audience engaged.

Know Your Audience

UNDERSTANDING YOUR audience's needs, interests, and expectations allows you to tailor your presentation accordingly. Here's how to get to know your audience:

- Research the Audience: Gather information about the audience's demographics, knowledge level, and interests. This will help you customize your content and delivery.

- Ask Questions: Start your presentation by asking questions to gauge the audience's interests and expectations.

- Use Relevant Examples: Use examples and anecdotes that resonate with the audience's experiences and interests.

Tell Stories

STORYTELLING IS A POWERFUL way to engage and connect with your audience. Here's how to incorporate stories into your presentation:

- Use Personal Stories: Share personal stories or experiences that relate to your topic. Personal stories create a connection and make your presentation more relatable.

- Create a Narrative Arc: Structure your stories with a clear beginning, middle, and end. Include a conflict or challenge and a resolution.

- Use Vivid Details: Use vivid details and descriptive language to bring your stories to life. Engage the audience's senses and emotions.

Incorporate Humor

HUMOR CAN LIGHTEN THE mood and make your presentation more enjoyable. Here's how to use humor effectively:

- Use Appropriate Humor: Ensure your humor is appropriate for the audience and the context. Avoid offensive or controversial jokes.

- Keep It Relevant: Use humor that is relevant to your topic and enhances your message.

- Be Natural: Deliver humor naturally and avoid forcing jokes. Authenticity is key to effective humor.

Encourage Interaction

ENCOURAGING INTERACTION keeps the audience engaged and involved. Here are some ways to promote interaction:

- Ask Questions: Ask open-ended questions to encourage audience participation. This can also help gauge their understanding and interest.

- Use Polls and Surveys: Use interactive tools, such as polls and surveys, to gather audience input and feedback.

- Facilitate Group Activities: Facilitate group discussions or activities that encourage collaboration and engagement.

Use Visual and Sensory Elements

INCORPORATING VISUAL and sensory elements can enhance engagement and retention. Here's how to use them effectively:

- Use High-Quality Visuals: Use high-quality images, videos, and graphics that support your message.

- Incorporate Sound and Music: Use sound effects or music to enhance your presentation and create a dynamic experience.

- Use Props and Demonstrations: Use props or demonstrations to illustrate key points and make your presentation more interactive.

4. Handling Nervousness and Building Confidence

EVEN SEASONED SPEAKERS experience nervousness. Handling nervousness and building confidence is key to delivering a successful presentation. Here are some strategies:

- Acknowledge Nervousness: Accept that feeling nervous is normal. Acknowledge your nervousness and focus on managing it.

- Prepare Thoroughly: Thorough preparation builds confidence. Knowing your material and practicing your delivery reduces anxiety.

- Visualize Success: Spend time visualizing yourself delivering a successful presentation. Imagine positive reactions from the audience and a sense of accomplishment.

- Focus on the Audience: Shift your focus from yourself to the audience. Concentrate on delivering value and connecting with them.

- Use Relaxation Techniques: Practice relaxation techniques, such as deep breathing and progressive muscle relaxation, to calm your nerves.

- Start Small: If you're new to public speaking, start with smaller, less intimidating audiences. Gradually build up to larger groups as your confidence grows.

5. Continuous Improvement

PUBLIC SPEAKING IS a skill that can always be improved. Here's how to continuously enhance your public speaking and presentation skills:

- Seek Feedback: Ask for feedback from trusted friends, colleagues, or mentors. Use their input to identify areas for improvement.

- Record and Review: Record your presentations and review them critically. Look for areas where you can improve your delivery, pacing, and engagement.

- Attend Workshops and Courses: Attend public speaking workshops and courses to learn new techniques and gain confidence.

- Join Speaking Clubs: Join organizations like Toastmasters to practice your speaking skills in a supportive environment and receive constructive feedback.

- Learn from Others: Watch and learn from accomplished speakers. Analyze their techniques, style, and delivery to gain insights and inspiration.

Personal Stories and Case Studies

TO ILLUSTRATE THE IMPACT of mastering public speaking and presentation skills, let's explore some personal stories and case studies.

Case Study 1: Sarah's Journey to Confident Public Speaking

SARAH, A 29-YEAR-OLD marketing manager, struggled with severe anxiety when speaking in public. She often felt overwhelmed and avoided opportunities to present in front of others. Sarah decided to work with a public speaking coach to overcome her fear and improve her skills.

Through coaching, Sarah learned to reframe her thoughts, visualize success, and practice relaxation techniques. She prepared thoroughly for her presentations by researching her material, creating a clear outline, and practicing regularly. Sarah also focused on engaging and connecting with her audience through storytelling and interaction.

Sarah's journey to confident public speaking led to significant improvements. She became more comfortable and composed in front of an audience, delivering impactful presentations with confidence. Her enhanced public speaking skills opened up new opportunities for career advancement and professional growth.

Case Study 2: Michael's Transformation through Effective Presentation Techniques

MICHAEL, A 35-YEAR-old software engineer, faced challenges in delivering clear and engaging presentations. He often struggled with organizing his content and connecting with his audience. Michael decided to attend a presentation skills workshop to enhance his abilities.

At the workshop, Michael learned techniques for preparing and delivering effective presentations. He focused on creating a clear outline, designing engaging visual aids, and practicing his delivery. Michael also incorporated storytelling, humor, and interaction to keep his audience engaged.

Michael's transformation was remarkable. He became more adept at organizing his content and delivering presentations that captivated his audience. His ability to engage and connect with his audience enhanced his professional reputation and career prospects.

Personal Story: Emily's Path to Engaging and Connecting with Her Audience

EMILY, A 27-YEAR-OLD teacher, struggled with engaging and connecting with her students during presentations. She often felt that her presentations were monotonous and failed to capture her students' attention. Emily decided to seek guidance from a mentor to improve her presentation skills.

Through mentoring, Emily learned the importance of knowing her audience, telling stories, and incorporating visual and sensory elements. She practiced using open-ended questions, interactive tools, and group activities to promote engagement. Emily also focused on using appropriate humor and varying her tone to maintain interest.

Emily's path to engaging and connecting with her audience led to significant improvements. She became more skilled at creating dynamic and interactive presentations that resonated with her students. Emily's journey to mastering public speaking and presentation skills enriched her teaching and personal growth.

CONCLUSION

Mastering public speaking and presentation skills is essential for personal and professional success. Overcoming the fear of public speaking, preparing and delivering effective presentations, and engaging and connecting with your audience are key components of this journey.

By understanding the roots of public speaking anxiety, changing your mindset, and using specific techniques to manage nervousness, you can build confidence and reduce anxiety. Thorough preparation, clear organization, and engaging delivery are crucial for delivering impactful presentations.

Personal stories and case studies demonstrate that transformation is possible with the right strategies and mindset. As you continue reading this book, remember that mastering public speaking and presentation skills is an ongoing journey that requires patience, practice, and self-compassion. By embracing this journey and applying the insights and techniques discussed, you can develop the public speaking and presentation skills needed to thrive in both personal and professional settings. Let's move forward together, step by step, towards more confident, engaging, and effective public speaking and presentations.

Chapter 12: Handling Social Rejection and Failure

Understanding that Rejection is a Part of Life

Rejection is an inevitable part of the human experience. Whether in personal relationships, professional settings, or social interactions, everyone faces rejection at some point. Understanding and accepting that rejection is a natural part of life can help individuals cope with it more effectively and use it as a stepping stone for growth and resilience.

1. The Universality of Rejection

Rejection is a universal experience. No one is immune to it, regardless of their status, achievements, or personality. Recognizing that rejection happens to everyone can help reduce the personal stigma and feelings of inadequacy that often accompany it. Famous figures from all walks of life have faced significant rejections before achieving success. For example, J.K. Rowling's manuscript for Harry Potter was rejected by numerous publishers before it became a global phenomenon.

2. Rejection as a Learning Experience

Rejection provides valuable feedback and opportunities for learning. Each rejection can offer insights into areas for improvement and growth. By viewing rejection as a learning experience, individuals can shift their perspective from seeing it as a failure to seeing it as a chance for development. This mindset encourages continuous self-improvement and resilience.

3. The Emotional Impact of Rejection

Rejection can evoke a range of emotions, including sadness, frustration, anger, and disappointment. It's essential to acknowledge and validate these emotions rather than suppress them. Understanding the emotional impact of rejection helps individuals process their feelings healthily and move forward constructively.

4. The Role of Rejection in Personal Growth

Rejection plays a crucial role in personal growth. It challenges individuals to reassess their goals, strategies, and behaviors. By embracing rejection, individuals can develop a stronger sense of self-awareness and resilience. Overcoming rejection fosters a growth mindset, where challenges are viewed as opportunities for learning and improvement.

Strategies for Coping with and Learning from Rejection

COPING WITH REJECTION involves developing strategies that allow individuals to process their emotions, learn from the experience, and move forward positively. The following strategies can help individuals cope with and learn from rejection.

1. Acknowledge and Validate Your Emotions

It's essential to acknowledge and validate your emotions when facing rejection. Allow yourself to feel sad, disappointed, or frustrated. Suppressing these emotions can lead to prolonged distress. Instead, give yourself permission to experience and express your feelings. This can be done through journaling, talking to a trusted friend, or engaging in creative outlets like art or music.

2. Reframe Your Perspective

Reframing your perspective involves viewing rejection as a temporary setback rather than a reflection of your worth. Here's how to reframe your perspective:

- See Rejection as Redirection: View rejection as a redirection toward better opportunities. Sometimes, rejection can lead you to paths that are more aligned with your true goals and values.

- Focus on Growth: Identify the lessons learned from the rejection and how they can contribute to your growth. Ask yourself, "What can I learn from this experience?" and "How can I improve?"

3. Practice Self-Compassion

Self-compassion involves treating yourself with kindness and understanding during times of rejection. Here are ways to practice self-compassion:

- Use Positive Affirmations: Replace self-critical thoughts with positive affirmations. For example, instead of thinking, "I'm not good enough," think, "I did my best, and I can learn from this experience."

- Be Kind to Yourself: Engage in self-care activities that nurture your well-being, such as taking a relaxing bath, going for a walk, or spending time with loved ones.

- Avoid Comparisons: Comparing yourself to others can exacerbate feelings of inadequacy. Focus on your unique journey and progress.

4. Seek Support

Seeking support from others can provide comfort and perspective during times of rejection. Here's how to seek support effectively:

- Talk to Trusted Friends or Family: Share your feelings and experiences with people who care about you. They can offer empathy, encouragement, and constructive feedback.

- Join Support Groups: Joining support groups, either in person or online, can connect you with others who have faced similar rejections. Sharing experiences and coping strategies can be empowering.

- Seek Professional Help: If rejection significantly impacts your mental health, consider seeking support from a therapist or counselor. They can provide guidance and tools for coping with rejection.

5. Develop Resilience

Resilience is the ability to bounce back from adversity and maintain a positive outlook. Building resilience involves developing skills and habits that enhance your ability to cope with rejection. Here's how to build resilience:

- Cultivate a Growth Mindset: Embrace challenges and view failures as opportunities for growth. A growth mindset fosters resilience by promoting adaptability and learning.

- Set Realistic Goals: Setting realistic and achievable goals helps build confidence and motivation. Break larger goals into smaller, manageable steps to maintain momentum.

- Practice Gratitude: Focus on the positive aspects of your life by practicing gratitude. Regularly reflecting on what you are thankful for can improve your overall well-being and resilience.

- Maintain a Healthy Lifestyle: Physical health and mental health are interconnected. Regular exercise, a balanced diet, and adequate sleep can enhance your resilience and ability to cope with stress.

6. Take Constructive Action

Taking constructive action involves using rejection as a catalyst for positive change. Here's how to take constructive action:

- Identify Areas for Improvement: Reflect on the reasons for the rejection and identify areas where you can improve. This could involve acquiring new skills, seeking feedback, or adjusting your approach.

- Set New Goals: Use the rejection as an opportunity to set new, meaningful goals. Focus on goals that align with your values and passions.

- Stay Persistent: Persistence is key to overcoming rejection. Keep pursuing your goals and dreams, even in the face of setbacks. Each rejection brings you one step closer to success.

7. Embrace the Power of Resilience

Embracing resilience involves recognizing your inner strength and capacity to overcome challenges. Here's how to embrace resilience:

- Celebrate Small Wins: Acknowledge and celebrate your achievements, no matter how small. Celebrating small wins can boost your confidence and motivation.

- Learn from Role Models: Look to role models who have overcome rejection and adversity. Their stories can provide inspiration and guidance for your journey.

- Stay Flexible and Adaptable: Be open to change and willing to adapt your strategies. Flexibility and adaptability are key components of resilience.

Building Resilience and Maintaining a Positive Outlook

BUILDING RESILIENCE and maintaining a positive outlook are essential for navigating rejection and failure. These qualities help individuals bounce back from setbacks and continue pursuing their goals with determination and optimism.

1. Cultivating a Positive Mindset

A positive mindset involves focusing on the opportunities and possibilities that arise from rejection and failure. Here's how to cultivate a positive mindset:

- Practice Positive Thinking: Challenge negative thoughts and replace them with positive affirmations. Focus on your strengths, achievements, and potential.

- Visualize Success: Spend time visualizing your goals and the steps needed to achieve them. Visualization can enhance motivation and confidence.

- Stay Optimistic: Maintain an optimistic outlook, even in the face of challenges. Believe in your ability to overcome obstacles and achieve your goals.

2. Building a Supportive Network

A supportive network provides encouragement, guidance, and resources during times of rejection and failure. Here's how to build a supportive network:

- Connect with Positive Influences: Surround yourself with people who inspire and uplift you. Positive influences can provide motivation and support.

- Seek Mentorship: Identify mentors who can offer advice and guidance based on their experiences. Mentors can provide valuable insights and help you navigate challenges.

- Join Communities: Join communities or groups that share your interests and goals. Being part of a community can provide a sense of belonging and support.

3. Developing Coping Skills

Effective coping skills help individuals manage stress and emotions during times of rejection and failure. Here's how to develop coping skills:

- Mindfulness and Meditation: Practice mindfulness and meditation to stay present and manage stress. These practices can enhance emotional regulation and resilience.

- Deep Breathing Exercises: Use deep breathing exercises to calm your mind and body. Deep breathing can reduce anxiety and promote relaxation.

- Journaling: Journaling allows you to express your thoughts and emotions in a safe space. It can provide clarity and help you process your experiences.

4. Setting Realistic Goals

SETTING REALISTIC GOALS helps maintain motivation and focus. Here's how to set realistic goals:

- Break Goals into Steps: Break larger goals into smaller, manageable steps. This makes the goals more achievable and less overwhelming.

- Set Specific and Measurable Goals: Set specific and measurable goals to track your progress. Clear goals provide direction and motivation.

- Celebrate Progress: Celebrate your progress and achievements along the way. Recognizing your accomplishments boosts confidence and encourages persistence.

5. Embracing Flexibility and Adaptability

Flexibility and adaptability are crucial for navigating rejection and failure. Here's how to embrace flexibility and adaptability:

- Be Open to Change: Embrace change and be willing to adjust your plans as needed. Flexibility allows you to adapt to new circumstances and opportunities.

- Learn from Experience: Use rejection and failure as learning experiences. Reflect on what worked and what didn't, and adjust your approach accordingly.

- Stay Resilient: Maintain resilience in the face of setbacks. Keep pursuing your goals with determination and adaptability.

6. Finding Meaning and Purpose

Finding meaning and purpose in your pursuits can provide motivation and resilience. Here's how to find meaning and purpose:

- Identify Your Values: Reflect on your values and passions. Align your goals and actions with your values to create a sense of purpose.

- Contribute to Others: Engaging in activities that benefit others can provide a sense of fulfillment and purpose. Volunteer, mentor, or support causes you care about.

- Stay Connected to Your Vision: Keep your long-term vision in mind. Staying connected to your vision provides motivation and direction.

7. Practicing Gratitude

Gratitude enhances well-being and resilience by focusing on the positive aspects of life. Here's how to practice gratitude:

- Keep a Gratitude Journal: Write down things you are grateful for each day. Reflecting on positive experiences fosters a positive outlook.

- Express Gratitude: Express gratitude to others for their support and kindness. Gratitude strengthens relationships and enhances well-being.

- Focus on the Present: Focus on the present moment and appreciate the small joys in life. Being present promotes mindfulness and gratitude.

Personal Stories and Case Studies

TO ILLUSTRATE THE IMPACT of handling social rejection and failure, let's explore some personal stories and case studies.

Case Study 1: John's Journey to Resilience

JOHN, A 35-YEAR-OLD graphic designer, faced significant rejection when his dream job application was turned down. He felt devastated and doubted his abilities. John decided to seek support from a career coach to build resilience and develop a positive outlook.

Through coaching, John learned to reframe his perspective and view rejection as an opportunity for growth. He practiced self-compassion, acknowledged his emotions, and focused on his strengths. John also set new goals and developed a plan to enhance his skills.

John's journey to resilience led to significant improvements. He became more confident and persistent in pursuing his career goals. John's positive outlook and resilience opened up new opportunities, and he eventually secured a position that aligned with his values and aspirations.

Case Study 2: Sarah's Transformation Through Learning from Failure

SARAH, A 28-YEAR-OLD entrepreneur, experienced failure when her startup business did not succeed. She felt overwhelmed and questioned her entrepreneurial abilities. Sarah decided to join a support group for entrepreneurs to learn from her experience and build resilience.

In the support group, Sarah learned to embrace failure as a learning experience. She practiced gratitude, focusing on the skills and knowledge she gained from her venture. Sarah also sought mentorship and guidance from experienced entrepreneurs.

Sarah's transformation was remarkable. She became more resilient and adaptable, using her failure as a stepping stone for growth. Sarah's positive outlook and determination led her to launch a new business, which achieved success and recognition in her industry.

Personal Story: Emily's Path to Overcoming Social Rejection

Emily, a 27-year-old teacher, faced social rejection when she was excluded from a social group at work. She felt isolated and questioned her social skills. Emily decided to seek guidance from a therapist to cope with rejection and build resilience.

Through therapy, Emily learned to acknowledge her emotions and practice self-compassion. She reframed her perspective, viewing rejection as an opportunity to build new connections. Emily also focused on her strengths and engaged in activities that brought her joy.

Emily's path to overcoming social rejection led to significant improvements. She became more confident in her social interactions and built meaningful relationships with supportive colleagues. Emily's resilience and positive outlook enriched her personal and professional life.

CONCLUSION

Handling social rejection and failure is an essential skill for personal and professional growth. Understanding that rejection is a part of life, developing strategies for coping with and learning from rejection, and building resilience and maintaining a positive outlook are key components of this journey.

By acknowledging and validating your emotions, reframing your perspective, practicing self-compassion, and seeking support, you can cope with rejection and use it as a catalyst for growth. Building resilience and maintaining a positive outlook involve cultivating a positive mindset, developing coping skills, setting realistic goals, embracing flexibility, finding meaning and purpose, and practicing gratitude.

Personal stories and case studies demonstrate that transformation is possible with the right strategies and mindset. As you continue reading this book, remember that handling rejection and failure is an ongoing journey that requires patience, practice, and self-compassion. By embracing this journey and applying the insights and techniques discussed, you can develop the resilience and positive outlook needed to thrive in both personal and professional settings. Let's move forward together, step by step, towards more resilient, positive, and fulfilling lives.

Chapter 13: Online Communication and Social Media

Navigating Digital Communication and Maintaining Social Confidence

In today's digital age, effective online communication is essential. From social media platforms to professional networking sites, digital communication has become a significant part of our daily lives. Navigating this landscape with confidence involves understanding the nuances of online interactions, maintaining a positive and professional presence, and balancing the digital and physical realms of communication.

1. Understanding the Dynamics of Digital Communication

DIGITAL COMMUNICATION differs from face-to-face interactions in several ways, and understanding these differences is crucial for maintaining social confidence online.

Lack of Non-Verbal Cues

ONE OF THE MOST SIGNIFICANT challenges of digital communication is the absence of non-verbal cues, such as facial expressions, tone of voice, and body language. These cues play a critical role in conveying emotions and intentions in face-to-face interactions. Without them, messages can be easily misinterpreted.

To mitigate this, use clear and concise language, and consider the context and potential interpretations of your messages. Emojis and punctuation can also help convey tone and emotion, but use them sparingly and appropriately based on the platform and audience.

Asynchronous Nature

DIGITAL COMMUNICATION often occurs asynchronously, meaning there can be a delay between sending and receiving messages. This can lead to misunderstandings and miscommunications.

To address this, be clear and specific in your messages. If a response is time-sensitive, indicate this clearly. Be patient with delays, and follow up politely if needed.

Public and Permanent Nature

CONTENT SHARED ONLINE can be both public and permanent. Once something is posted, it can be difficult to retract or erase entirely, and it may be visible to a broad audience.

Before posting, consider the potential long-term impact of your words and actions. Maintain a professional and respectful tone, and avoid sharing sensitive or personal information publicly.

2. Building and Maintaining Social Confidence Online

MAINTAINING SOCIAL confidence online involves being authentic, engaging positively with others, and presenting yourself professionally. Here are strategies to help you build and maintain social confidence in digital communication.

Authenticity and Honesty

AUTHENTICITY IS KEY to building trust and credibility online. Be honest and transparent in your communications. Share your true thoughts and experiences, and avoid presenting a false or exaggerated image of yourself.

Positive Engagement

ENGAGE POSITIVELY WITH others by showing respect, kindness, and empathy. Avoid negative or confrontational language, and strive to contribute constructively to discussions. Recognize and celebrate others' achievements, and offer support and encouragement.

Professionalism

Maintain a professional demeanor, especially on platforms related to work or industry. Use proper grammar and punctuation, and avoid slang or overly casual language. Present yourself in a way that reflects your values and goals.

3. Strategies for Effective Online Communication

EFFECTIVE ONLINE COMMUNICATION requires careful consideration of the platform, audience, and message. Here are strategies to enhance your digital communication skills.

Tailor Your Communication to the Platform

DIFFERENT PLATFORMS have different norms and expectations. Tailor your communication style to suit the platform you are using. For example:

- Email: Use a formal tone, proper salutations, and clear subject lines. Be concise and to the point.

- Social Media: Use a more casual and conversational tone. Engage with visual content, such as images and videos, to capture attention.

- Professional Networking Sites: Maintain a professional tone and focus on industry-related content. Share insights, articles, and updates relevant to your field.

Be Clear and Concise

CLARITY AND CONCISENESS are crucial in online communication. Avoid long-winded explanations or ambiguous language. Use bullet points or numbered lists to organize information clearly. Ensure your message is easy to read and understand.

Proofread and Edit

PROOFREAD AND EDIT your messages before sending or posting. Check for spelling and grammatical errors, and ensure your message is coherent and professional. This extra step can prevent misunderstandings and enhance your credibility.

Respect Privacy and Confidentiality

RESPECT THE PRIVACY and confidentiality of others in your digital communications. Avoid sharing sensitive or personal information without permission. Use private messaging for confidential conversations, and be mindful of the audience when posting publicly.

4. Handling Negative Interactions

NEGATIVE INTERACTIONS, such as online criticism or conflict, are inevitable in digital communication. Handling these situations with grace and confidence is essential.

Stay Calm and Composed**

WHEN FACED WITH NEGATIVE interactions, stay calm and composed. Avoid reacting impulsively or defensively. Take a moment to assess the situation before responding.

Address the Issue Constructively

ADDRESS THE ISSUE CONSTRUCTIVELY by acknowledging the other person's perspective and providing a thoughtful response. Focus on finding a resolution rather than escalating the conflict.

Use Private Channels

FOR SENSITIVE OR PERSONAL issues, use private messaging or direct communication channels. This can prevent public confrontations and allow for more productive discussions.

Know When to Disengage

NOT ALL NEGATIVE INTERACTIONS require a response. Know when to disengage from unproductive or hostile exchanges. Protect your well-being by avoiding unnecessary stress and negativity.

Building a Positive Online Presence

A POSITIVE ONLINE PRESENCE is crucial for personal branding and professional success. It involves curating content that reflects your values, skills, and goals, engaging with your audience, and maintaining consistency across platforms.

1. Personal Branding

PERSONAL BRANDING INVOLVES presenting yourself in a way that highlights your unique strengths, experiences, and aspirations. Here's how to build a strong personal brand online.

Define Your Brand

START BY DEFINING YOUR personal brand. Consider the following questions:

- What are your core values and beliefs?

- What skills and expertise do you want to highlight?

- What are your career goals and aspirations?

- What unique experiences or perspectives do you bring?

Use these insights to create a clear and consistent message that represents your brand.

Create a Professional Profile

CREATE PROFESSIONAL profiles on relevant platforms, such as LinkedIn, Twitter, or a personal website. Ensure your profiles are complete and up-to-date, including a professional photo, a compelling bio, and detailed information about your experience and achievements.

Showcase Your Work

SHOWCASE YOUR WORK and accomplishments through portfolio pieces, project highlights, or case studies. Use visual content, such as images, videos, and infographics, to make your work more engaging and accessible.

Share Valuable Content

SHARE VALUABLE CONTENT that aligns with your brand and interests. This could include articles, blog posts, videos, or industry insights. Sharing valuable content positions you as a thought leader and attracts engagement from your audience.

2. Engaging with Your Audience

ENGAGING WITH YOUR audience involves interacting with others in a meaningful and positive way. Here's how to build and maintain engagement.

Be Responsive

RESPOND TO COMMENTS, messages, and inquiries promptly. Acknowledge and appreciate feedback, and engage in conversations with your audience.

Participate in Discussions

PARTICIPATE IN DISCUSSIONS related to your field or interests. Share your insights and perspectives, ask questions, and engage with others' content.

Collaborate with Others

COLLABORATE WITH OTHERS in your industry or community. This could involve guest blogging, joint projects, or social media takeovers. Collaboration expands your reach and fosters valuable connections.

Celebrate and Support Others

CELEBRATE AND SUPPORT others' achievements and milestones. Recognize and share others' work, and offer encouragement and support.

3. Maintaining Consistency Across Platforms

CONSISTENCY ACROSS platforms ensures that your online presence is cohesive and recognizable. Here's how to maintain consistency.

Use a Consistent Visual Identity

USE CONSISTENT VISUAL elements, such as colors, fonts, and logos, across all platforms. This creates a cohesive and professional appearance.

Align Your Messaging

ENSURE THAT YOUR MESSAGING is consistent across platforms. Use a similar tone and style in your communications, and reinforce your core values and brand message.

Regularly Update Your Profiles

REGULARLY UPDATE YOUR profiles with new information, achievements, and content. Keeping your profiles current reflects your ongoing growth and engagement.

Monitor Your Online Presence

MONITOR YOUR ONLINE presence to ensure consistency and accuracy. Use tools to track mentions, reviews, and engagement, and address any discrepancies or issues promptly.

Balancing Online and Offline Interactions

BALANCING ONLINE AND offline interactions is essential for maintaining social confidence and overall well-being. While digital communication offers numerous benefits, face-to-face interactions provide unique advantages that cannot be replicated online.

1. The Benefits of Face-to-Face Interactions

FACE-TO-FACE INTERACTIONS offer several benefits that enhance social connections and communication.

Non-Verbal Communication

FACE-TO-FACE INTERACTIONS allow for the full range of non-verbal communication, including facial expressions, body language, and tone of voice. These cues enhance understanding and empathy.

Building Stronger Relationships

IN-PERSON INTERACTIONS often lead to deeper and more meaningful relationships. The shared physical presence and immediate feedback foster stronger connections.

Improved Collaboration

FACE-TO-FACE INTERACTIONS facilitate better collaboration and problem-solving. The ability to communicate and respond in real-time enhances teamwork and innovation.

Emotional Support

IN-PERSON INTERACTIONS provide a higher level of emotional support. Physical presence and touch, such as a hug or handshake, can convey comfort and reassurance.

2. Integrating Online and Offline Interactions

INTEGRATING ONLINE and offline interactions involves leveraging the strengths of both to build and maintain strong relationships.

Use Online Communication to Initiate Connections

USE ONLINE COMMUNICATION to initiate and build connections. Social media and networking platforms provide opportunities to connect with people you might not meet in person.

Transition to Face-to-Face Meetings

WHENEVER POSSIBLE, transition online connections to face-to-face meetings. Meeting in person can deepen relationships and enhance trust.

Combine Digital and Physical Engagement

COMBINE DIGITAL AND physical engagement for a comprehensive approach to relationship-building. For example, follow up online interactions with phone calls, video chats, or in-person meetings.

Maintain Regular In-Person Interactions

MAKE AN EFFORT TO MAINTAIN regular in-person interactions with friends, family, and colleagues. Schedule coffee meetings, lunch dates, or social gatherings to stay connected.

3. Managing Screen Time and Digital Detox

MANAGING SCREEN TIME and incorporating digital detoxes can help maintain a healthy balance between online and offline interactions.

Set Boundaries

SET BOUNDARIES FOR screen time and online activities. Designate specific times for checking emails, social media, and other digital tasks.

Take Regular Breaks

TAKE REGULAR BREAKS from screens to rest your eyes and mind. Use these breaks to engage in physical activities, spend time outdoors, or connect with others in person.

Practice Digital Detox

INCORPORATE DIGITAL detoxes into your routine. Designate specific times or days to disconnect from digital devices and focus on offline activities.

Prioritize Offline Activities

PRIORITIZE OFFLINE activities that bring you joy and fulfillment. Engage in hobbies, exercise, and spend quality time with loved ones.

Personal Stories and Case Studies

TO ILLUSTRATE THE IMPACT of navigating online communication and social media, building a positive online presence, and balancing online and offline interactions, let's explore some personal stories and case studies.

Case Study 1: Jane's Journey to a Positive Online Presence

JANE, A 32-YEAR-OLD graphic designer, struggled with presenting herself professionally online. She often felt unsure about how to engage with her audience and build her personal brand. Jane decided to work with a personal branding coach to enhance her online presence.

Through coaching, Jane learned to define her personal brand, create a professional profile, and share valuable content. She focused on showcasing her work, engaging positively with her audience, and maintaining consistency across platforms.

Jane's journey to a positive online presence led to significant improvements. She became more confident in her digital communication, attracted new clients, and built a strong professional reputation. Jane's enhanced online presence contributed to her career growth and personal fulfillment.

Case Study 2: Michael's Transformation Through Balancing Online and Offline Interactions

MICHAEL, A 35-YEAR-old software engineer, faced challenges in balancing his online and offline interactions. He often felt overwhelmed by screen time and disconnected from in-person relationships. Michael decided to seek guidance from a life coach to improve his balance.

Through coaching, Michael learned to set boundaries for screen time, prioritize offline activities, and integrate online and offline interactions. He practiced digital detoxes, scheduled regular in-person meetings, and combined digital and physical engagement.

Michael's transformation was remarkable. He became more connected with his friends, family, and colleagues, and experienced improved well-being. Michael's ability to balance online and offline interactions enriched his personal and professional life.

Personal Story: Emily's Path to Navigating Digital Communication with Confidence

EMILY, A 27-YEAR-OLD teacher, struggled with navigating digital communication and maintaining social confidence online. She often felt anxious about how her messages would be perceived and found it challenging to engage effectively. Emily decided to seek support from a digital communication coach to build her confidence.

Through coaching, Emily learned to understand the dynamics of digital communication, tailor her messages to different platforms, and handle negative interactions with grace. She focused on being authentic, engaging positively, and maintaining professionalism.

Emily's path to navigating digital communication with confidence led to significant improvements. She became more adept at online interactions, built a positive online presence, and balanced her digital and physical communication effectively. Emily's journey to mastering digital communication enriched her personal and professional relationships.

Conclusion

Navigating online communication and social media, building a positive online presence, and balancing online and offline interactions are essential skills in today's digital age. By understanding the dynamics of digital communication, maintaining social confidence, and leveraging the strengths of both online and offline interactions, individuals can build meaningful connections and achieve personal and professional success.

Maintaining a positive online presence involves defining your personal brand, engaging with your audience, and ensuring consistency across platforms. Balancing online and offline interactions requires integrating digital and physical engagement, managing screen time, and prioritizing offline activities.

Personal stories and case studies demonstrate that transformation is possible with the right strategies and mindset. As you continue reading this book, remember that mastering online communication and social media is an ongoing journey that requires patience, practice, and self-compassion. By embracing this journey and applying the insights and techniques discussed, you can develop the digital communication skills needed to thrive in both personal and professional settings. Let's move forward together, step by step, towards more confident, engaging, and effective online communication and social media presence.

Chapter 14: Continuous Improvement and Practice

The Importance of Continuous Practice in Social Skill Development

Social skills, like any other skill set, require continuous practice and refinement. While some people may naturally excel in social situations, others might need more deliberate effort to develop these skills. Continuous practice not only helps in mastering social interactions but also ensures that these skills remain sharp and adaptable to various contexts.

1. The Nature of Social Skills

Social skills encompass a wide range of abilities, including communication, empathy, relationship-building, conflict resolution, and more. These skills are not static; they evolve with experience and practice. Effective social skills enable individuals to navigate different social environments, from casual gatherings to professional settings, with confidence and ease.

2. The Role of Practice in Skill Development

Practice is essential for embedding social skills into everyday behavior. Here's why continuous practice is crucial:

- Reinforcement: Repeated practice reinforces new behaviors and habits, making them more natural and automatic.

- Feedback and Adjustment: Practice allows for real-time feedback and adjustments, helping to refine and improve skills.

- Confidence Building: Regular practice boosts confidence by reducing anxiety and increasing familiarity with different social scenarios.

- Adaptability: Continuous practice enhances adaptability, enabling individuals to apply their skills in various contexts and with diverse groups of people.

3. Overcoming Social Anxiety

For individuals with social anxiety, continuous practice is particularly important. Facing social situations repeatedly can help desensitize anxiety triggers and build a sense of mastery over time. Techniques such as gradual exposure, cognitive-behavioral strategies, and mindfulness can be integrated into practice routines to support anxiety reduction.

4. The Benefits of Lifelong Learning

Social skill development is a lifelong journey. Embracing a mindset of lifelong learning encourages individuals to seek new experiences, challenge themselves, and continually grow. Lifelong learning in social skills can lead to richer, more fulfilling relationships and greater success in personal and professional endeavors.

Creating Opportunities for Social Interaction

CREATING AND SEEKING out opportunities for social interaction is key to continuous practice. These opportunities can be found in everyday life, structured environments, and through deliberate efforts to engage with others.

1. Everyday Opportunities

Everyday interactions provide numerous opportunities to practice social skills. Here are some examples:

- Casual Conversations: Engage in casual conversations with neighbors, colleagues, or strangers in places like cafes, parks, and public transport.

- Social Gatherings: Attend social gatherings such as parties, community events, or family functions. Use these settings to practice initiating conversations, active listening, and building rapport.

- Workplace Interactions: Use interactions with colleagues, clients, and supervisors to practice professional communication, collaboration, and networking.

2. Structured Environments

Structured environments offer more formal settings for social skill development. Here are some options:

- Workshops and Seminars: Attend workshops and seminars on topics of interest. These events provide opportunities to network, participate in group discussions, and engage with speakers.

- Clubs and Organizations: Join clubs, organizations, or professional associations related to your interests or industry. These groups offer regular meetings and activities that facilitate social interaction.

- Classes and Courses: Enroll in classes or courses that involve group work or interactive sessions. Learning environments can be a great place to meet new people and practice social skills.

3. Deliberate Efforts

Making deliberate efforts to create social opportunities involves seeking out and initiating interactions. Here's how:

- Volunteering: Volunteer for community service projects, charity events, or local organizations. Volunteering not only provides social interaction but also a sense of purpose and fulfillment.

- Organizing Events: Organize events or gatherings, such as game nights, book clubs, or networking events. Taking the initiative to host events can enhance your social skills and leadership abilities.

- Joining Interest Groups: Join groups or clubs centered around hobbies or interests, such as sports teams, hiking groups, or creative workshops. Shared interests provide common ground for building connections.

4. Virtual Opportunities

In today's digital age, virtual opportunities for social interaction are abundant. Here's how to leverage them:

- Online Communities: Join online communities or forums related to your interests. Participate in discussions, share insights, and connect with like-minded individuals.

- Virtual Events: Attend virtual events, webinars, and conferences. Use chat features, breakout rooms, and social media to engage with other attendees.

- Social Media: Use social media platforms to connect with friends, family, and professionals. Engage in conversations, share content, and participate in online groups.

Setting Long-Term Goals for Social Growth

SETTING LONG-TERM GOALS for social growth provides direction, motivation, and a sense of purpose in your social skill development journey. Here's how to set and achieve meaningful long-term goals.

1. Identifying Areas for Improvement

Start by identifying areas where you want to improve your social skills. Reflect on your strengths and weaknesses, and consider feedback from others. Common areas for improvement include:

- Communication Skills: Enhancing clarity, assertiveness, and active listening.

- Relationship-Building: Building deeper, more meaningful connections.

- Conflict Resolution: Managing and resolving conflicts effectively.

- Empathy and Understanding: Developing greater empathy and understanding of others.

2. Setting SMART Goals

SMART goals are Specific, Measurable, Achievable, Relevant, and Time-bound. Here's how to set SMART goals for social growth:

- Specific: Clearly define what you want to achieve. For example, "I want to improve my public speaking skills."

- Measurable: Establish criteria to measure your progress. For example, "I will give three presentations in the next six months."

- Achievable: Ensure your goal is realistic and attainable. For example, "I will join a local Toastmasters club to practice my speaking skills."

- Relevant: Make sure your goal aligns with your overall objectives. For example, "Improving public speaking will enhance my career prospects."

- Time-bound: Set a deadline for achieving your goal. For example, "I will achieve this goal by the end of the year."

3. Developing a Plan of Action

Once you have set your goals, develop a plan of action to achieve them. Here's how:

- Break Down Goals: Break down larger goals into smaller, manageable steps. This makes the goals less overwhelming and more achievable.

- Identify Resources: Identify the resources and support you need to achieve your goals. This could include books, courses, mentors, or support groups.

- Create a Timeline: Create a timeline for completing each step of your plan. Set deadlines for each milestone to stay on track.

4. Tracking Progress

Tracking your progress is essential for staying motivated and making adjustments as needed. Here's how to track your progress effectively:

- Keep a Journal: Keep a journal to document your experiences, challenges, and achievements. Reflecting on your progress helps you stay focused and motivated.

- Set Regular Check-Ins: Set regular check-ins to review your progress. This could be monthly or quarterly, depending on your goals.

- Seek Feedback: Seek feedback from trusted friends, mentors, or colleagues. They can provide valuable insights and help you identify areas for improvement.

5. Celebrating Achievements

Celebrating your achievements, no matter how small, is crucial for maintaining motivation and a positive outlook. Here's how to celebrate your achievements:

- Acknowledge Milestones: Acknowledge and celebrate each milestone you reach. This reinforces your progress and encourages continued effort.

- Reward Yourself: Reward yourself for achieving your goals. This could be through a special treat, a fun activity, or simply taking time to relax and reflect.

- Share Your Success: Share your achievements with others. Celebrating with friends, family, or colleagues can enhance your sense of accomplishment and build supportive relationships.

6. Adapting and Adjusting Goals

As you progress, you may need to adapt and adjust your goals. Life circumstances, new experiences, and changing priorities can impact your goals. Here's how to adapt and adjust effectively:

- Stay Flexible: Be open to adjusting your goals and plans as needed. Flexibility allows you to adapt to new opportunities and challenges.

- Reassess Regularly: Reassess your goals regularly to ensure they remain relevant and achievable. Make adjustments based on your progress and evolving priorities.

- Stay Committed: Stay committed to your long-term vision, even if you need to adjust your goals. Persistence and dedication are key to achieving lasting social growth.

Personal Stories and Case Studies

TO ILLUSTRATE THE IMPACT of continuous improvement and practice in social skill development, creating opportunities for social interaction, and setting long-term goals for social growth, let's explore some personal stories and case studies.

Case Study 1: John's Journey to Social Confidence

JOHN, A 35-YEAR-OLD software developer, struggled with social anxiety and found it challenging to engage in social interactions. He often avoided social gatherings and felt isolated. John decided to seek support from a therapist to improve his social skills and build confidence.

Through therapy, John learned techniques for managing his anxiety and gradually exposing himself to social situations. He set specific goals, such as initiating conversations with colleagues and attending social events. John practiced these skills regularly and sought feedback from his therapist.

John's journey to social confidence led to significant improvements. He became more comfortable in social settings, built meaningful relationships, and experienced increased confidence and well-being. John's commitment to continuous practice and setting long-term goals contributed to his social growth and personal fulfillment.

Case Study 2: Sarah's Transformation Through Social Interaction Opportunities

SARAH, A 28-YEAR-OLD marketing manager, felt that her social skills were underdeveloped due to her introverted nature. She often felt disconnected from her colleagues and struggled to build a professional network. Sarah decided to join a local professional association to create opportunities for social interaction.

Through the association, Sarah attended workshops, seminars, and networking events. She practiced her social skills by engaging in conversations, participating in group discussions, and volunteering for committees. Sarah also set long-term goals to build a strong professional network and enhance her communication skills.

Sarah's transformation was remarkable. She became more adept at navigating social interactions, built a robust professional network, and experienced career growth. Sarah's deliberate efforts to create social interaction opportunities and set long-term goals contributed to her social skill development and professional success.

Personal Story: Emily's Path to Continuous Social Growth

EMILY, A 27-YEAR-OLD teacher, wanted to enhance her social skills to build stronger relationships with her students and colleagues. She often felt that her interactions were superficial and lacked depth. Emily decided to seek guidance from a mentor to develop a plan for continuous social growth.

Through mentoring, Emily identified areas for improvement, such as active listening, empathy, and conflict resolution. She set SMART goals and developed a plan of action, including attending professional development courses and participating in team-building activities. Emily tracked her progress through journaling and regular check-ins with her mentor.

Emily's path to continuous social growth led to significant improvements. She became more effective in her communication, built deeper connections with her students and colleagues, and experienced greater job satisfaction. Emily's commitment to continuous improvement and setting long-term goals enriched her personal and professional life.

Conclusion

Continuous improvement and practice are essential for social skill development. By understanding the importance of practice, creating opportunities for social interaction, and setting long-term goals for social growth, individuals can enhance their social skills and build meaningful relationships.

Maintaining a mindset of lifelong learning, seeking feedback, and celebrating achievements contribute to ongoing social development. Personal stories and case studies demonstrate that transformation is possible with the right strategies and mindset.

As you continue reading this book, remember that social skill development is an ongoing journey that requires patience, practice, and self-compassion. By embracing this journey and applying the insights and techniques discussed, you can develop the social skills needed to thrive in both personal and professional settings. Let's move forward together, step by step, towards more confident, engaging, and fulfilling social interactions.

Chapter 15: Real-Life Success Stories

Inspiring Stories of Individuals Who Overcame Shyness

Shyness can be a significant barrier to personal and professional success. However, many individuals have overcome their shyness and transformed their lives in remarkable ways. This chapter shares inspiring stories of such individuals, highlighting the lessons learned from their journeys and offering encouragement and motivation for readers to embark on their own paths.

1. John's Journey: From Shy Teenager to Public Speaker

JOHN WAS A SHY TEENAGER who often avoided social interactions. He struggled with making friends and participating in class discussions. His shyness made him feel isolated and hindered his academic and social development. However, John was determined to overcome his shyness and build his confidence.

Early Struggles and Breakthrough

JOHN'S BREAKTHROUGH came during his senior year of high school when he was encouraged by his English teacher to join the debate team. Initially hesitant, John decided to take the challenge. His first few debates were nerve-wracking, but with each session, he became more comfortable speaking in front of an audience.

Building Confidence Through Practice

JOHN PRACTICED REGULARLY, honing his debating skills and learning to articulate his thoughts clearly. He also sought feedback from his coach and peers, which helped him improve. Over time, John's confidence grew, and he began to enjoy public speaking.

Embracing Public Speaking

AFTER HIGH SCHOOL, John continued to pursue public speaking opportunities. He joined Toastmasters, a public speaking club, where he further developed his skills and gained confidence. John eventually became a sought-after speaker, sharing his journey from shyness to confidence with others.

Lessons Learned

JOHN'S JOURNEY TEACHES us the importance of stepping out of our comfort zones and embracing challenges. Regular practice, seeking feedback, and persistence are key to overcoming shyness and building confidence.

2. Sarah's Transformation: From Introverted Engineer to Team Leader

SARAH WAS AN INTROVERTED engineer who preferred working alone and avoided social interactions. Her shyness limited her career growth, as she struggled with networking and presenting her ideas in meetings. Determined to advance in her career, Sarah decided to work on her social skills.

Recognizing the Need for Change

SARAH RECOGNIZED THAT her shyness was holding her back professionally. She enrolled in a communication skills workshop to learn effective communication strategies and techniques for building rapport with colleagues.

Taking Small Steps

SARAH STARTED BY TAKING small steps to improve her social skills. She initiated conversations with colleagues, participated in team meetings, and sought opportunities to collaborate on projects. These small interactions helped her build confidence and develop stronger relationships with her peers.

Seeking Mentorship

SARAH SOUGHT MENTORSHIP from a senior engineer who had overcome similar challenges. Her mentor provided guidance, support, and valuable insights into navigating social interactions in the workplace. This mentorship played a crucial role in Sarah's transformation.

Achieving Leadership Roles

WITH IMPROVED COMMUNICATION skills and increased confidence, Sarah began to take on leadership roles within her team. She led projects, presented at conferences, and mentored junior engineers. Her ability to connect with others and articulate her ideas made her a respected and influential leader.

Lessons Learned

SARAH'S STORY HIGHLIGHTS the importance of recognizing the need for change and taking proactive steps to improve social skills. Seeking mentorship and taking small, consistent actions can lead to significant personal and professional growth.

3. Emily's Evolution: From Anxious Student to Confident Teacher

EMILY WAS AN ANXIOUS student who found it challenging to speak up in class or participate in group activities. Her shyness affected her academic performance and social life. Determined to overcome her anxiety, Emily sought help from a therapist and embarked on a journey of self-discovery and growth.

Therapy and Self-Reflection

THROUGH THERAPY, EMILY gained a deeper understanding of her anxiety and its triggers. She learned coping strategies, such as mindfulness and deep breathing exercises, to manage her anxiety in social situations.

Self-reflection helped her identify areas for improvement and set realistic goals for personal growth.

Joining Support Groups

EMILY JOINED SUPPORT groups for individuals with social anxiety. These groups provided a safe space to share experiences, practice social interactions, and receive encouragement from others facing similar challenges. The support and camaraderie she found in these groups were instrumental in her progress.

Pursuing a Career in Teaching

DESPITE HER SHYNESS, Emily had a passion for teaching. She pursued a degree in education and worked on building her confidence through student teaching experiences. With each teaching opportunity, Emily became more comfortable speaking in front of a class and engaging with students.

Becoming a Confident Educator

EMILY'S DEDICATION and hard work paid off. She became a confident and effective teacher, known for her ability to connect with students and create a positive learning environment. Emily now mentors other teachers who struggle with shyness and anxiety, sharing her journey and insights.

Lessons Learned

EMILY'S JOURNEY UNDERSCORES the importance of seeking professional help, joining support groups, and pursuing passions despite fear and anxiety. Consistent effort and self-reflection can lead to significant transformation and fulfillment.

4. Michael's Story: From Reserved Accountant to Networking Pro

MICHAEL WAS A RESERVED accountant who found it difficult to network and build professional relationships. His shyness limited his career opportunities and prevented him from advancing in his field. Determined to overcome his shyness, Michael decided to work on his networking skills.

Joining Professional Associations

MICHAEL JOINED PROFESSIONAL associations and attended networking events to practice his social skills. Initially, he felt uncomfortable and anxious, but he pushed himself to engage in conversations and build connections.

Developing a Networking Strategy

MICHAEL DEVELOPED A networking strategy that included setting specific goals for each event, such as meeting a certain number of new people or collecting business cards. He prepared conversation starters and practiced active listening to build rapport with others.

Seeking Feedback and Continuous Improvement

MICHAEL SOUGHT FEEDBACK from colleagues and mentors on his networking approach. He used this feedback to refine his strategy and improve his social interactions. Continuous improvement and practice helped him become more confident and effective in networking.

Achieving Career Advancement

WITH IMPROVED NETWORKING skills, Michael built a strong professional network that opened up new career opportunities. He received job offers, invitations to speak at industry events, and recognition for his contributions to the field. Michael's ability to connect with others and build relationships significantly advanced his career.

Lessons Learned

MICHAEL'S STORY DEMONSTRATES the importance of developing a strategy, seeking feedback, and continuously improving social skills. Networking can be a powerful tool for career advancement and personal growth.

5. Lisa's Transformation: From Socially Awkward Teen to Community Leader

LISA WAS A SOCIALLY awkward teenager who struggled with making friends and fitting in. Her shyness made her feel isolated and unaccepted. Determined to change her social dynamics, Lisa decided to take proactive steps to improve her social skills and build a sense of belonging.

Joining Extracurricular Activities

LISA JOINED EXTRACURRICULAR activities at school, such as the drama club and student council. These activities provided opportunities to interact with peers, build confidence, and develop leadership skills. Participating in group projects and performances helped Lisa step out of her comfort zone and gain social experience.

Volunteering and Community Involvement

LISA ALSO GOT INVOLVED in volunteering and community service. She volunteered at local shelters, organized fundraisers, and participated in community events. Volunteering allowed Lisa to connect with diverse groups of people and develop empathy and communication skills.

Building a Support Network

LISA BUILT A SUPPORT network of friends, mentors, and community members who encouraged and supported her growth. This network provided a sense of belonging and helped Lisa navigate social challenges.

Becoming a Community Leader

WITH IMPROVED SOCIAL skills and increased confidence, Lisa took on leadership roles in her community. She organized events, led initiatives, and advocated for causes she cared about. Lisa's ability to connect with others and inspire action made her a respected community leader.

Lessons Learned

LISA'S TRANSFORMATION highlights the importance of getting involved in activities, volunteering, and building a support network. Taking proactive steps to engage with others can lead to personal growth, confidence, and a sense of belonging.

Lessons Learned from Their Journeys

THE JOURNEYS OF JOHN, Sarah, Emily, Michael, and Lisa provide valuable lessons for anyone looking to overcome shyness and build social confidence. Here are some key takeaways from their stories:

1. Embrace Challenges

Stepping out of your comfort zone and embracing challenges is essential for growth. Whether it's joining a debate team, attending networking events, or volunteering, taking on new experiences helps build confidence and develop social skills.

2. Practice Regularly

Continuous practice is crucial for embedding social skills into everyday behavior. Regular practice, whether through casual conversations or structured environments, reinforces new behaviors and builds confidence over time.

3. Seek Support and Mentorship

Seeking support from friends, mentors, and professionals can provide valuable guidance and encouragement. Mentorship offers insights and advice from those who have overcome similar challenges, while support groups provide camaraderie and shared experiences.

4. Develop a Strategy

Having a clear strategy for social interactions can help reduce anxiety and increase effectiveness. Setting specific goals, preparing conversation starters, and practicing active listening are practical strategies for building social confidence.

5. Focus on Continuous Improvement

Continuous improvement and self-reflection are key to long-term growth. Seeking feedback, tracking progress, and making adjustments based on experiences help refine social skills and build resilience.

6. Pursue Passions and Interests

Pursuing passions and interests can provide a sense of purpose and fulfillment. Engaging in activities you enjoy allows you to connect with like-minded individuals and build meaningful relationships.

7. Build a Support Network

Building a support network of friends, mentors, and community members provides encouragement, guidance, and a sense of belonging. A strong support network can help navigate social challenges and celebrate achievements.

Encouragement and Motivation for Readers to Embark on Their Own Paths

OVERCOMING SHYNESS and building social confidence is a journey that requires patience, practice, and persistence. The stories of John, Sarah, Emily, Michael, and Lisa demonstrate that transformation

is possible with the right strategies and mindset. Here are some final words of encouragement and motivation for readers to embark on their own paths:

1. Believe in Yourself

Believe in your ability to overcome shyness and build social confidence. Everyone has the potential for growth and transformation. Trust yourself and take the first step towards positive change.

2. Take Small Steps

Start with small, manageable steps. Whether it's initiating a conversation, attending a social event, or joining a club, each small step builds confidence and momentum. Celebrate your progress along the way.

3. Embrace Imperfection

Perfection is not the goal. Embrace imperfection and view mistakes as opportunities for learning and growth. Every experience, whether successful or challenging, contributes to your development.

4. Seek Support

Don't be afraid to seek support from friends, mentors, or professionals. Support and encouragement from others can provide motivation and guidance on your journey.

5. Stay Persistent

Persistence is key to overcoming shyness and building social confidence. Keep pushing yourself, even when faced with setbacks or challenges. Each step forward brings you closer to your goals.

6. Celebrate Your Achievements

Acknowledge and celebrate your achievements, no matter how small. Celebrating your progress reinforces your efforts and encourages continued growth.

7. Inspire Others

Your journey can inspire others facing similar challenges. Share your experiences, offer support, and be a source of encouragement for those around you.

CONCLUSION

The real-life success stories of individuals who overcame shyness and built social confidence provide valuable lessons and inspiration. By embracing challenges, practicing regularly, seeking support, and focusing on continuous improvement, anyone can achieve personal and professional growth.

The journeys of John, Sarah, Emily, Michael, and Lisa demonstrate that transformation is possible with determination and the right strategies. As you continue reading this book, remember that your journey is unique, and you have the potential to achieve your goals and build meaningful relationships.

Embrace the journey, take small steps, seek support, and stay persistent. Your path to social confidence and fulfillment awaits. Let these stories inspire and motivate you to embark on your own journey of growth and transformation. Together, step by step, we can overcome shyness, build social confidence, and create a life filled with meaningful connections and success.

Conclusion

Recap of Key Points Covered in the Book

AS WE REACH THE CONCLUSION of this book, it is valuable to reflect on the key points and strategies discussed throughout the chapters. This book has been a comprehensive guide to developing social confidence and effective communication skills, aiming to empower readers to navigate social interactions with ease and authenticity.

1. Understanding Social Confidence

In the opening chapters, we explored the definition of social confidence and its profound impact on both personal and professional life. Social confidence is not merely about being extroverted or outgoing; it encompasses the ability to engage with others, express oneself clearly, and build meaningful relationships. We also debunked common misconceptions about social skills and shyness, emphasizing that these abilities can be developed and honed through deliberate practice.

2. The Psychology of Shyness

We delved into the psychological underpinnings of shyness, examining its genetic, environmental, and psychological causes. Understanding the relationship between shyness and social anxiety provided a foundation for developing strategies to manage these feelings. Recognizing that shyness is a common experience and not an insurmountable barrier was crucial in framing our approach to overcoming it.

3. Self-Awareness and Self-Esteem

Building self-awareness and healthy self-esteem were highlighted as essential components of social confidence. Techniques for increasing self-awareness, such as mindfulness and reflection, were discussed, along with strategies for building and maintaining self-esteem. Understanding oneself better allows for more authentic and confident interactions with others.

4. Developing Social Skills

We explored core social skills necessary for effective communication, including active listening, verbal and non-verbal communication, and empathy. Techniques for improving these skills were provided, with an emphasis on practice and feedback. Developing these foundational skills is crucial for building strong, positive relationships.

5. Overcoming Social Anxiety

Practical strategies for managing and reducing social anxiety were a focal point in the book. Cognitive-behavioral techniques for challenging negative thoughts, along with mindfulness and relaxation exercises, were introduced. These tools help individuals face social situations with greater calm and confidence.

6. Building Self-Confidence

We discussed the role of self-confidence in social interactions and provided exercises and activities to boost self-confidence. Setting and achieving personal goals for social growth was emphasized as a way to build a sense of accomplishment and motivation.

7. Effective Conversation Techniques

Effective conversation techniques, such as starting and sustaining conversations, asking questions, and showing genuine interest, were covered in detail. Making meaningful connections through dialogue was underscored as a key aspect of social confidence.

8. Non-Verbal Communication Mastery

Understanding and mastering non-verbal communication, including body language, facial expressions, and gestures, was highlighted. Tips for improving one's own body language and reading others' non-verbal cues were provided to enhance communication effectiveness.

9. Social Etiquette and Manners

The importance of social etiquette in various contexts, guidelines for polite and respectful interactions, and adapting etiquette to different social situations were explored. Social etiquette helps in creating a positive impression and fostering respectful relationships.

10. Networking and Building Relationships

Strategies for effective networking and building and maintaining professional relationships were discussed. The role of trust and reciprocity in strong connections was emphasized, along with practical tips for networking success.

11. Public Speaking and Presentation Skills

Overcoming the fear of public speaking, techniques for preparing and delivering effective presentations, and engaging and connecting with the audience were covered. These skills are essential for professional success and personal growth.

12. Handling Social Rejection and Failure

Understanding that rejection is a part of life and developing strategies for coping with and learning from rejection were key points. Building resilience and maintaining a positive outlook were highlighted as crucial for overcoming setbacks and continuing to pursue social growth.

13. Online Communication and Social Media

Navigating digital communication and maintaining social confidence online were discussed. Building a positive online presence and balancing online and offline interactions were emphasized to ensure a well-rounded approach to social communication.

14. Continuous Improvement and Practice

The importance of continuous practice in social skill development, creating opportunities for social interaction, and setting long-term goals for social growth were explored. Continuous improvement is essential for maintaining and enhancing social confidence.

15. Real-Life Success Stories

Inspiring stories of individuals who overcame shyness and built social confidence provided real-world examples of the principles discussed in the book. Lessons learned from their journeys and encouragement for readers to embark on their own paths were provided.

Encouragement to Apply Learned Skills in Daily Life

THE STRATEGIES AND techniques discussed in this book are not meant to be theoretical concepts but practical tools that you can apply in your daily life. Here are some ways to incorporate these skills into your everyday interactions:

1. Practice Regularly

Social skills, like any other skill, require regular practice. Make a conscious effort to engage in social interactions, whether at work, in your community, or with friends and family. Use everyday opportunities to practice active listening, effective conversation techniques, and non-verbal communication.

2. Set Realistic Goals

Set specific, achievable goals for your social growth. These could include attending a certain number of social events each month, initiating conversations with new people, or joining a club or organization. Regularly review and adjust your goals as you make progress.

3. Reflect and Adjust

Reflect on your social interactions and identify areas for improvement. Seek feedback from trusted friends or mentors and use it to refine your skills. Continuous reflection and adjustment are key to ongoing improvement.

4. Embrace Challenges

Don't shy away from social challenges. Whether it's speaking in public, attending a networking event, or engaging in a difficult conversation, embrace these opportunities as chances to grow and build confidence.

5. Stay Positive and Resilient

Maintaining a positive outlook and resilience is crucial for social growth. Celebrate your successes, learn from your setbacks, and keep moving forward. Remember that social confidence is a journey, not a destination.

6. Seek Support

Don't hesitate to seek support from friends, family, mentors, or professionals. Having a support system can provide encouragement, guidance, and motivation as you work on developing your social skills.

Final Thoughts and Words of Motivation for Continuous Improvement

AS YOU EMBARK ON YOUR journey to build social confidence and improve your communication skills, remember that progress takes time and effort. Be patient with yourself and celebrate every step forward, no matter how small. Here are some final thoughts and words of motivation to keep you inspired:

1. Believe in Your Potential

You have the potential to develop strong social skills and build meaningful relationships. Believe in your ability to grow and succeed. Your efforts will pay off, and you will see positive changes in your interactions and relationships.

2. Embrace Growth Mindset

Adopt a growth mindset, where challenges and setbacks are viewed as opportunities for learning and improvement. Embrace the process of continuous growth and be open to new experiences and perspectives.

3. Stay Committed

Commit to your personal and social growth. Consistency and dedication are key to developing lasting social confidence. Keep practicing, reflecting, and adjusting your approach as needed.

4. Inspire Others

Your journey can inspire others who face similar challenges. Share your experiences, offer support, and encourage those around you. Your success can motivate others to embark on their own paths to social confidence.

5. Enjoy the Journey

Enjoy the journey of self-discovery and growth. Building social confidence is not just about achieving specific goals but also about enjoying the process and the connections you make along the way.

Appendix

Additional Resources for Further Reading

TO CONTINUE YOUR JOURNEY of social skill development and communication improvement, here are some additional resources for further reading:

Books:

1. "How to Win Friends and Influence People" by Dale Carnegie

2. "The Charisma Myth: How Anyone Can Master the Art and Science of Personal Magnetism" by Olivia Fox Cabane

3. "Quiet: The Power of Introverts in a World That Can't Stop Talking" by Susan Cain

4. "Crucial Conversations: Tools for Talking When Stakes Are High" by Kerry Patterson, Joseph Grenny, Ron McMillan, and Al Switzler

5. "Daring Greatly: How the Courage to Be Vulnerable Transforms the Way We Live, Love, Parent, and Lead" by Brené Brown

Websites:

1. [Toastmasters International](https://www.toastmasters.org) - A nonprofit educational organization that teaches public speaking and leadership skills through a worldwide network of clubs.

2. [Mind Tools](https://www.mindtools.com) - Offers resources on various soft skills, including communication, leadership, and personal development.

3. [Psychology Today](https://www.psychologytoday.com) - Provides articles and resources on mental health, relationships, and personal growth.

4. [TED Talks](https://www.ted.com/talks) - Features inspiring talks by experts on a wide range of topics, including communication and personal development.

5. [The School of Life](https://www.theschooloflife.com) - Offers resources and courses on emotional intelligence, relationships, and personal growth.

Worksheets and Exercises for Practicing Social Skills

THE FOLLOWING WORKSHEETS and exercises can help you practice and improve your social skills:

1. Active Listening Worksheet:

- Objective: Practice active listening skills in conversations.

- Instructions: During a conversation, focus on the speaker and use the following prompts to guide your listening:

- Make eye contact and nod occasionally to show engagement.

- Avoid interrupting and allow the speaker to finish their thoughts.

- Paraphrase what the speaker said to confirm understanding.

- Ask open-ended questions to encourage further discussion.

- Reflect on the conversation afterward and note areas for improvement.

2. Conversation Starters Exercise:

- Objective: Develop confidence in initiating and sustaining conversations.

- Instructions: Prepare a list of conversation starters to use in different social situations. Practice using these starters in real interactions. Examples include:

- "What brought you to this event?"

- "What do you enjoy most about your job?"

- "Have you read any interesting books lately?"

- "What are your favorite hobbies?"

3. Social Goals Planner:

- Objective: Set and track social goals for continuous improvement.

- Instructions: Use the planner to set specific, achievable social goals. Break down each goal into smaller steps and set deadlines for completion. Track your progress and celebrate achievements. Example template:

- Goal: Improve public speaking skills

- Steps:

1. Join a local Toastmasters club (Deadline: Month 1)

2. Prepare and deliver a speech (Deadline: Month 2)

3. Seek feedback and refine speech (Deadline: Month 3)

- Progress Tracking:

- Joined Toastmasters club (Completed: Month 1)

- Delivered first speech (Completed: Month 2)

- Received feedback and made improvements (Completed: Month 3)

4. Reflection Journal:

- Objective: Reflect on social interactions and identify areas for growth.

- Instructions: Keep a daily or weekly journal to reflect on your social interactions. Note what went well, what challenges you faced, and what you learned. Use these reflections to set new goals and strategies for improvement.

5. Non-Verbal Communication Practice:

- Objective: Improve non-verbal communication skills.

- Instructions: Practice using positive body language, facial expressions, and gestures in everyday interactions. Use a mirror or record yourself to observe and refine your non-verbal cues. Focus on the following:

- Maintain good posture and open body language.

- Make appropriate eye contact.

- Use gestures to emphasize points.

- Smile and use facial expressions to convey emotions.

List of Recommended Books and Websites

HERE IS A LIST OF RECOMMENDED books and websites to further enhance your social skills and personal growth:

Books:

1. "The Art of Conversation: Change Your Life with Confident Communication" by Judy Apps

2. "The Assertiveness Workbook: How to Express Your Ideas and Stand Up for Yourself at Work and in Relationships" by Randy J. Paterson

3. "The Gifts of Imperfection: Let Go of Who You Think You're Supposed to Be and Embrace Who You Are" by Brené Brown

4. "Emotional Intelligence: Why It Can Matter More Than IQ" by Daniel Goleman

5. "Social Intelligence: The New Science of Human Relationships" by Daniel Goleman

Websites:

1. [Coursera](https://www.coursera.org) - Offers online courses on communication, social skills, and personal development from top universities and institutions.

2. [Skillshare](https://www.skillshare.com) - Provides a variety of online classes on public speaking, networking, and other social skills.

3. [Khan Academy](https://www.khanacademy.org) - Features educational resources and courses on a wide range of topics, including personal growth and soft skills.

4. [LinkedIn Learning](https://www.linkedin.com/learning) - Offers professional development courses on communication, leadership, and other skills.

5. [Verywell Mind](https://www.verywellmind.com) - Provides articles and resources on mental health, relationships, and personal development.

AS YOU CONCLUDE YOUR journey through this book, remember that the path to social confidence and effective communication is ongoing. Embrace the process, stay committed to your growth, and continue applying the skills you have learned. Your efforts will lead to richer, more fulfilling relationships and greater success in all areas of your life. Thank you for joining me on this journey, and I wish you all the best in your pursuit of social confidence and personal growth.

Don't miss out!

Visit the website below and you can sign up to receive emails whenever Timothy Scott Phillips publishes a new book. There's no charge and no obligation.

https://books2read.com/r/B-A-KCQWC-FOTJF

BOOKS2READ

Connecting independent readers to independent writers.

About the Author

Timothy Scott Phillips is a dedicated author specializing in non-fiction self-help books that empower readers to overcome challenges and embrace personal growth. With a passion for mental health, resilience, and self-improvement, Timothy combines research-based insights with practical strategies to inspire lasting change. His work reflects a deep commitment to helping individuals navigate life's complexities, build confidence, and unlock their full potential. When he's not writing, Timothy enjoys mentoring, exploring nature, and connecting with his readers to share stories of transformation and hope. His books are a testament to the power of perseverance and the human spirit.

www.ingramcontent.com/pod-product-compliance
Ingram Content Group UK Ltd.
Pitfield, Milton Keynes, MK11 3LW, UK
UKHW031011181224
452569UK00001B/156